WORSHIP AND SECULAR MAN

DATE DUE			

WORSHIP AND SECULAR MAN

An essay on the liturgical nature of man, considering Secularization as a major phenomenon of our time and Worship as an apparent fact of all times. A study towards an integral anthropology.

by

Raimundo Panikkar

ORBIS BOOKS
MARYKNOLL. NEW YORK

DARTON, LONGMAN & TODD
London

Darton, Longman & Todd Ltd
85 Gloucester Road, London SW7 4SU

Orbis Books
Maryknoll, New York 10545

First published 1973

217

P19w

91204

Dec. 1974

Library of Congress Catalog Card No. 72–93339

ISBN 0 232 51191 8 (Great Britain).

*Produced by computer-controlled phototypesetting,
using OCR input techniques, and printed offset in Great Britain by
UNWIN BROTHERS LIMITED
The Gresham Press, Old Woking, Surrey*

CONTENTS

PREFACE

Man cannot live without rites. He cannot do without worship, even though secular man today may not be inspired by the traditional forms of worship. Secular man does not find his own balance in turning again to a number of more or less esoteric or for him exotic cults. The waves of secularisation seem to be receding. New forms of the sacred seem to be in their foam. But the ocean is neither wave nor foam only. Man is always more and also less of what he himself thinks himself to be.

This essay, which undeniably reflects—and refracts—an autobiographical itinerancy, took origin in a paper presented to a consultation, 'Worship in a Secular Age', organised by the World Council of Churches in 1969. Though revised and enlarged, this anthropological reflection is, however, neither a whole systematic treatise nor does it say that man is secular man only, thus depriving him of his multi-dimensional complexity. This study is critical but not iconoclastic. And in our times of paper-inundation and word-inflation, this brief book is presupposedly laconic. It insinuates only and leaves examples and explanations to the reader. The author remembers those old and wise words of the *Tao Te ching*

> "When the Way (*Tao*) fades away, virtue (*Te*) raises up,
> When virtue fades away, humanness (*jēn*) raises up,
> When humanness fades away, justice (*yi*) raises up,
> When justice fades away, the ritual (*li*) raises up,
> Ritual is but the mere crust of loyalty and good faith,
> And the beginning of discord."

R. Panikkar
Santa Barbara, Calif.
November 3, 1972.

INTRODUCTION

1. THE PROBLEM

No mathematician would dare to tackle an equation with three unknowns in it. Theologians hardly agree upon the very concept of *worship* (in the New Testament alone there are over 30 cultic expressions); philosophers discuss endlessly the meaning and, even more, the value of *secularization*; and now we want to relate these two already problematic factors so as to elaborate the even more fragile concept of *"worship in a secular age"*. But life is not mathematics and perhaps the effort to clarify z may help us incidentally to discover a more precise meaning for x and y.

The possibility of such an enterprise is ultimately based on the fact that everything in the world is interrelated and that beings themselves are nothing but relations. If such is the case, the study of a particular and in some ways new relationship may shed light on two concepts which, because they were kept in separation and seen as incompatible, were almost on the verge of death.

To put forward my thesis straightaway: only worship can prevent secularization from becoming inhuman, and only secularization can save worship from being meaningless. But for this to be proven, both concepts may not only have to be analysed but dynamically transformed.

If worship is something with a universal value and not merely tied to a particular form of culture or religion, in

1

other words, if worship is a constitutive human dimension, then it must have some meaning in a secularized society and this meaning has to be discovered or, if needs be, re-forged.

If secularization, for better or for worse, exists as an historical (and thus a real) situation for at least an important sector of mankind, it has to come to grips with one of the most widespread cultural phenomena of all times, i.e. worship.

In a word, the meeting and eventual clash between these two factors is today unavoidable.

We must be aware, that in this necessary encounter and dialogue a total risk is involved, i.e. that the theology of worship may eliminate or anathematize secularization, as being the main evil confronting man; or that secularism may have to get rid of worship as being a remnant of an age dead and gone. But again I insist that the dialogue is vital and—precisely because of this—fraught with mortal danger to both sides.

Since the problem is, in addition, so vast and this essay only intended to promote further study and stimulate discussion, I am bound to limit myself to certain aspects of the question, and more specifically to the *and* which relates the two concepts.

After attempting a working definition of the two terms, the relationship of which we should like to examine, we shall approach the problem from a threefold perspective. The *first* will be *methodological.* This perspective will show us that a merely *a posteriori* approach is in this case constitutively insufficient and that we shall have to discover in what we call the 'symbolic difference' the necessary criteria for doing justice to the problem itself. But the very nature of our problem will lead us to recognise that a vital issue like that of worship in a secular age cannot ultimately be

2

'planned' or postulated by any conscious, rational method: we have to leave room for the Spirit, allowing for growth and inspiration, both of which resist any manipulation even by the best intentioned mind. The domain of freedom has to be really free and no amount of philosophical or theological speculation, although necessary, is sufficient to explain or to dictate a spontaneous and vital human situation.

The *second* perspective (Chapter 2) will be the *philosophical* one. Relying on a more universal scheme, which we consider not merely valid but effective and which does violence to neither the facts nor the theories, we intend to introduce a certain intelligibility to the problem of worship throughout the ages but against a background of data furnished by the History of Religions; we shall not, however, have time to bother with details. The anthropological and philosophical patterns of heteronomy, autonomy and ontonomy will help us in this second part to lay some foundations for a possible theology of worship in a secular age.

The *third* perspective (Chapter 3) is the theological one, understanding the term theology in a broad and universal sense, though having in mind more the Western, Christian background for it is in this historical and geographical area that the problem has become most acute. We shall here develop the 'principle of complementarity' with its corollary of 'universality and concreteness' for these categories not only aid our understanding but actually point to a path which might well lead to a fruitful balance of theory and practice. In the last section of this third chapter we intend to develop a number of structures in which authentic worship could grow and perhaps even flourish in our time.

What gives fundamental unity to this essay is our endeavour to establish an integral anthropology. It is in fact an attempt at affirming the liturgical nature of man, thus considering worship to be an essential human dimension, while, at the same time, recognizing secularization to be a major phenomenon of our age, a phenomenon which, from now on, is assuredly destined to assist the growth of man's consciousness. To-day, anyone who is not exposed to secularization cannot hope to realise his humanity to the full, at least not in terms of the 20th century. On the other hand, man without worship cannot even subsist. Yet, for far too long these elements have been regarded as totally incompatible. We intend to study their reconciliation, not by postulating a general theory, but by trying to clarify the immediate, concrete and thus more universal aspects of the problem.

This anthropological basis is also the reason why we do not rely as heavily as most writers on the sociological aspect. This is not because we think it irrelevant, but rather because we consider the social aspect of man to be an integral part of the human being as a person. Throughout this essay, we make a fundamental distinction between individual and person.

Whereas an 'individual' is the opposite of 'society', a 'person' is not. It is understandable that, in reaction to the individualistic attitude adopted to many problems, contemporary writers tend to stress the sociological factors involved. But this dichotomy between individual and society is unnecessary if we start from an integral anthropology, which does not consider man as an individual but as a person and sees society not as a sum of individuals but as the natural, personal field of human interaction.

An individual is a practical, pragmatic, and artificial abstraction, i.e., the concept of 'individual' appears when we have cut away the living relationships of a human being and reduced him to a unit which can be seized and manipulated, a unit which is limited by the body, or rather by what some cultures would call the gross-body. A person, on the other hand does not finish at his finger-nails and cannot be reduced to his gross-matter. A person is real, present and alive wherever that person is loved, is heard, is seen, is influential, is effective. A person is a bundle of relationships, which cross at a certain centre which we may call personality, or even, if we insist, individuality, but this centre can in no way be regarded as synonymous for a person. An individual can have a number and even a weight, but a person cannot. An individual can be selfish for selfishness can, perhaps, be advantageous to him; for a person selfishness is unthinkable. An individual is a separated entity with a relationship to society that is extrinsic or democratic whereas person and society are not antagonistic. Every person is society for the whole gamut of personal pronouns can be applied to him.

Be that as it may, when we speak of worship and relate it to the human person, we should bear in mind that we are neither defending an individualistic idea of worship nor propounding a merely collectivistic notion of it. Worship is a human value and, as such, a personal one and can, thus neither be considered an affair of the individual nor of the community alone.

This essay is also intended to be a contribution to the study of comparative religion, if by that we do not simply mean a 'comparison of religions', but the illumination of one or more religious problems with the help of more than one religious tradition.

The highly concise form of this study will explain and I hope excuse the absence of foot-notes and references. I can only assure the reader that, as with an iceberg, so nine tenths of this essay lie beneath the surface.

2. WORSHIP

The word worship has hardly any equivalent in other European languages. Cult may be the nearest synonym; all the other Romance or Germanic words have a much more restricted meaning.

The English word worship is extremely vague and includes a number of actions, which probably have little meaning for us to-day. Thus, whereas, sacrifice and meditation have maintained their importance, words like entreaty and supplication have lost a great deal of their former significance.

Etymologically, the word comes from *weorp*, i.e. *worth*, value, and thus stands for esteem, honour. From this it has acquired the meaning of importance, respect, dignity and so on (cf. the German word 'Wurde'). From the beginning, the word had religious connotations: veneration of a power considered divine, reverence for a superior being, adoration, etc. Significantly, the etymological and probably most original meaning of 'worth' is 'economic value': it is the price of something. We show, then, respect to somebody or render reverent homage, because we have discovered that the object of our worship has value for us.

There have been a great many definitions of worship, some of quite recent origin, yet, properly speaking, the word worship is only a generic term, for it includes more than a dozen fundamentally different human attitudes.

As it is not our main purpose to analyse the different forms of worship, we must simply content ourselves by recalling generic words like cult, rite, service, religion, piety, religiousness, etc., together with more specific terms like sacrifice, prayer, adoration, reverence, devotion, invocation, aspiration, homage, supplication, rogation, intercession, orison, petition, oblation, libation, thanksgiving, praise, veneration, consecration, unction,

6

impetration, celebration, meditation, surrender, contemplation, love, etc. Let us also recall, just to remind ourselves of the complexity of our theme, that according to Scholastic theology, the sacrifice of the Mass with its four elements of communion, sacrifice, eucharist and memorial, has five effects: namely adoration (*latreia*), thanksgiving (*eucharistia*), prayer (*impetratio*), forgiveness (*propitiatio*), and satisfaction (*satisfactio*).

If worship includes all these groups of phenomena, it is indeed a decidedly comprehensive concept. However, even the most cursory review of the terms mentioned would show that practically all of them present the same basic structure: an act of the person by which he or she enters into contact with something or somebody that is transcendent and superior in order either to give or receive something material or spiritual. But we may perhaps leave the linguistic analysis for another occasion.

In an attempt to sum up the various opinions and perspectives I shall venture to define worship as the *expression of a belief*, or rather more accurately, by worship I understand any *human action symbolizing a belief*: to be still more precise, worship is any *symbolical act arising from a particular belief*. Let me explain.

By the word *expression* we mean an *action*, something which the worshipper does. Now, if the act which symbolizes the belief is considered to be an act of the intellect, worship will take an intellectual form and thus be related to such things as concentration, meditation, recognition, truthfulness, and the like. If the symbolic act is that of the will or the heart, then worship will be related to acts like devotion, surrender, love, praise, and the like. If a man's external actions are considered the truest expression of his beliefs then worship will be related to feast, celebration, dance and the like. If however, a man's most worthy actions are constructive and performed for the sake of his fellow men worship will be connected with ideas of service, work, duty and the like.

Furthermore, if a belief is not considered well expressed unless expressed collectively, then worship will be considered to be essentially the work of a community. If, on the other hand, the expression of belief is held to be the intimate experience of one person, worship will take the form of an internal act.

Similarly, if a belief is only considered to have been fully expressed when re-enacted in a particular way, then that re-enactment will be regarded as the most sublime form of religious worship. (We may well recall, for instance, that martyrdom was once considered to be the perfect form of worship).

Not every action is worship, but only those which are considered to be expressions of a belief, i.e. manifestations of religion, if we agree in calling religion the locus of belief.

Worship is a *symbolic act*. This means that it is neither a purely private act, expressing the psychological or subjective intention of the worshipper, nor a merely objective action which contains noetically what it expresses.

A symbolic act is an act that transcends its own immediate action, i.e., it contains an intention which goes beyond that of the people involved. What I am saying may be the same as affirming that worship is a sacrament in the broadest sense of the term, a symbolic act carrying with it, and thus neither in the mind of the worshipper *only*, nor in the 'objectifiable' act alone, a peculiar weight, a particular *glory*, one could add, recalling that the Hebrew word *kâbôd*, means both weight and glory.

8

Introduction

Worship is an act giving expression to a *belief*. I here take belief to mean religious belief, leaving aside the problem of whether there are, properly speaking, any non-religious beliefs. By belief I understand a particular crystallization of faith, a particular human response to faith and thus—because man is a thinking being—a certain conceptualization of faith, a set of fundamental tenets in which a particular religion claims to embody its message. Beliefs are beside and beyond the words expressing them, but yet not totally independent of them. I consider *faith*, on the other hand, a universal phenomenon, a constitutive dimension of man and, we might add, his existential openness to the transcendent, that is, if we agree not necessarily to interpret this term along purely ontological lines. If faith is a human dimension, it does not allow of any plurality. Now, the *act* of faith is the response of the human being to faith and because the human person is an intellectual being this act will have a predominantly intellectual dimension. The particular *act* by which man responds to his faith is what I would like to call belief. There is only one faith as there is only one reason; however there are as many beliefs as there are systems of philosophy, these being constructions of reason aiming at giving an account of reality and our place in it. But at present we do not need to follow up this idea further.

To sum up: any act of worship is an act of faith, i.e. an expression of belief (whereas we leave open the question of whether all expressions of faith could be said to be acts of worship).

3. SECULARIZATION

Secularization is also another polyvalent and ambiguous concept. To discover its underlying unity, we may follow the different uses and translations of the word. It is most probably of Etruscan origin, and related to the latin 'sero', 'serare', to sow, to plant, to generate, to scatter. From there it came to mean 'generation' and thus a 'phase', a period. The *saeculum* is not simply the world, and certainly not the *kosmos,* but rather its temporal aspect: the *aiôn.* But each translation contains a new shift of meaning. As we know, *aiôn* means life-span (cf. the Sanskrit *âyus* and its many compounds with the same meaning), though philosophical language as early as Parmenides took it to express the specific manner of existence of beings: the great philosophical controversy being whether this 'temporal' manner of existence is proper to Being or is only the sign of Becoming. '*Olam* in Hebrew also means time and world, or rather it stands for this, the temporal world.

Secular means, therefore, the temporal world, the temporal aspect of reality. Now, the different meanings and evaluations of the secular will depend on the particular conception of time that is being expressed.

If the temporal aspect is considered to have a negative connotation, *saeculum* will mean the so-called secular world as distinct from the sacred world which is regarded as ultimately important and real. The secular will then be the temporal. Now the temporal is the transient and thus not the everlasting: in consequence, it is not worthy of absorbing all our efforts. Secularization will then be the process of invading the realm of the sacred, the mystical, the religious, the assumption being that these latter terms stand for what is permanent and thus the non-temporal.

If, on the other hand, the temporal is considered to have a positive connotation, *saeculum* will stand as a symbol for regaining or conquering the realm of the real, monopolized previously by the sacred and the religious. Secularization will then be the liberation of mankind from the grip of obscurantism: the secular man will be the full human being assuming his responsibilities, the secular state will consist in human corporate living over and above the sectarian ways of the different religions, and secularism will be the ideal state of humanity.

In a word, the process of secularization is connected with ever increasing importance being given to time and the temporal.

For our purpose it may suffice to consider secularization as an ever recurrent human process which has repeatedly manifested itself in almost all cultures and which now forms a profound and constant part of our own cultural situation. Indeed, in the light of modern secularization the sphere of the sacred which is identified with the non-temporal, is being reduced more and more, tending in some areas even to disappear altogether.

If the secular has been identified with the temporal and differently valued in accordance with the evaluation of temporal reality, the sacred, taken here as synonymous with the non-secular, has traditionally been identified with the non-temporal, the word being here taken in a positive sense. Now, what is emerging in our days, and what may be a 'hapax phenomenon', a unique occurrence in the history of mankind, is—paradoxically—not secularism, but the sacred quality of secularism. In other words, what seems to be unique in the human constellation of the present *kairos* is the disruption of the equation sacred-non-temporal together with the positive value so far attached to it. The temporal is seen today as positive and, in a way, sacred. The secular man does not need to be anti-religious or anti-sacred, for he stands for the positive and, in a way, sacred value of time and temporal reality.

To sum up: The process of secularization corresponds to that degree of human consciousness which discovers the positive and at the same time real character of time and temporal reality. Traditional attitudes to time fluctuate between the experience of it as either a real entity without positive value, or an unreal entity with positive value. In other words different cultures and religions have considered time to be either something good, but not ultimately real, not definitive, not important because only a means to something else—or they have considered time the only reality, the definitive status, but negative, full of suffering and vanity, to say the least. In our days a new attitude is emerging: this considers time to be both positive and definitive, good and final, not a means that one can manipulate or a period which one has to go through, but an end in itself and the only real mode of existence. It is not by chance that today only mystics can understand the language of the secular.

Disregarding for our present purpose theological refinements and exceptional phenomena in the world of spirituality we could perhaps sum up the main outlines of man's attitude towards time like this:

$$
\text{time} \begin{cases} \text{unreal} \begin{cases} \text{negative: Hindu Religions.} \\ \text{positive: Buddhism.} \end{cases} \\ \\ \text{real} \begin{cases} \text{negative: Semitic Religions.} \\ \text{positive: Secular attitude.} \end{cases} \end{cases}
$$

This is another version of the old metaphysical dilemma: either God is real and the world is not real (insofar as God is real, the problem of evil, for instance, can be solved at the price of denying its ontological reality), or God is not real because the world is real and there is no place for duality. Secularization is the process

12

of the penetration of 'reality' into the world, the process of making the world real, which according to different interpretations will amount to saying: sacred, divine, or, on the contrary, more independent, more itself, more world, and ultimately real.

The specific character of our investigation advises us not to pursue this matter farther, lest we break the balance of our study.

Chapter 1

CRITERIA FOR AN ANSWER

Methodological Considerations

1. INSUFFICIENT CRITERIA

There is an attitude which, with the best of intentions, tries to focus attention on the problem from the point of view of pastoral theology or apologetics. In a rather pointed form, the argument runs rather like this:

'Modern man has lost his taste for worship, has evolved another set of values and feelings which make him a stranger to the—traditional—world of worship. Let us accommodate ourselves to his ways, make worship as beautiful and attractive as possible and study how we can best convey its message and lead him again to a life of worship.' This attitude may invoke lofty principles like *lex suprema salus animarum*, 'the sabbath is made for man and not man for the sabbath', 'to worship God in spirit and in truth', etc. but is, nevertheless, based on the uncritical conviction that we already have the solution and the problem is merely one of presenting it in a more palatable way.

I would like to call this attitude the mentality of the *translators*: we have to translate they tell us, i.e. move from the pulpit to the altar, from Gregorian chant to modern jazz, from the sacred to the profane, from the boring to the exciting, from the clerics to the laity, from the temples to the houses, from the confessional to the ecumenical and so on. Many more examples could be given for, indeed, they abound.

To be sure, the translators have done a marvellous job, and have been pioneers of many a badly needed reform. Many of the modifications they have introduced are extremely valuable and they have saved many a congregation and perhaps even a Church from crumbling under the overwhelming weight of tradition. I am not passing any value judgement on such reforms. I am only saying: a) that this attitude is ultimately inadequate and b) that this criterion is insufficient.

(a) The attitude is ultimately inadequate for it rests on a rather weird pragmatic assumption: the old devices did not work, or at least they do not work now, so let us experiment with new procedures. This attitude is betrayed not only in the examples suggested above, but also in the language used: to find better ways to convey the message, to proclaim the entrusted treasure, to clothe, translate, adapt, accommodate and the like. Perhaps the most irritating expression is one which has crept into high ecclesiastical spheres: 'experimental liturgies'; as if one could experiment with the liturgy as one does with white mice in a laboratory, in order to see if something 'works', as if one could experiment with love just to see if it satisfies, as if the Christian sacrifice done 'experimentally' were a kind of 'dry mass' to test the reaction of the people, as if the liturgy could be manipulated to this extent.

Certainly, none of the people concerned are doing this intentionally and they would, no doubt, agree with my criticisms but that is just what confirms my fear, namely that they act in this unconscious way simply because they take for granted precisely that which should be examined and critically re-thought: the very meaning and the

15

essence of worship, the content and not only the forms, the substance and not the accidentals, the real meaning and not the connotations. Pragmatism is not altogether wrong, but in this case it is obviously insufficient, for we are not leaning on a healthy confidence in nature, man or reality, but dealing with something which is by no means a primeval datum.

This leads me already to my second reason for challenging the attitude of the translator.

(b) The criterion is insufficient for it is uncritical regarding the core of the problem. If worship constitutes a problem in our secularised society, the principle reason is not that the liturgy is out-moded or boring (it was almost equally so two hundred years ago), but rather that the principles of the liturgy itself are in crisis. Fashion or boredom are not the main obstacles but the fear of meaninglessness.

All too often theological reflection about this problem remains superficial, considering it mainly as a practical or pastoral problem, while basically it is theological. I maintain that worship or liturgy is the most important theological issue of Christianity today and perhaps of all religions. Is not worship religion *qua* religion in action? Is it not due to this lack of an adequate theology of worship that Christian organizations and churches today so often officially engage in social, economic, political and similar activities and enter into competition with parallel secular agencies, so that any difference and thus any justification for duplicating the work is blurred? The present situation may represent an understandable reaction against the other-worldliness of religions and their traditional indifference when confronted with the problems of the world. Tired of 'praying to God' as a substitute for acting humbly, of 'asking divine mercy' instead of being merciful, of praising an unconcerned and apparently indifferent Supreme Being instead of extolling and enhancing human potentialities, an essentially Christian and religious spirit has impelled scores of the most serious men and women of our time to get rid of what they regard as merely an obsolete piece of paraphernalia and devote themselves to the immediate service of the world.

We have to tackle this problem in all its seriousness and not just think we have nothing else to do once we have castigated oddities and exaggerations. Furthermore, I am convinced that the question cannot be answered by a mere compromise.

To-day, it is unlikely that anyone with a reasonably developed mind will be satisfied with the dualistic answer that the one thing (sacred worship) has to be performed as well as the other (secular work), that there is time for everything, and that work should respect worship just as worship should not interfere with work. Martha and Mary were not strangers but sisters and probably lived in the same house. After all, Mary did choose only one '*part*', though the best. Contemporary man wants the whole and not simply one part. The same Hebrew work ('*abad*) which means work, service, also means worship. The whole of the secular becomes sacred; nothing is more sacred than the secular. But let us proceed in order.

Any criterion based on mere adaptation or simple translation is thus insufficient, because it takes for granted that which is being challenged, namely, the very meaning of worship as sacred action over against secular work.

2. NECESSARY CRITERIA
If the working definition of worship given at the

17

beginning is valid, it may furnish us with a criterion to discriminate between authentic and non-authentic forms of worship. What does not express the belief of a person, a community or a religion can no longer be considered an authentic form of worship. In this case the living ritual has degenerated into deadly ritualism. When the act has ceased to be the carrier of the symbolism which gives life and meaning to it, when it has ceased to be a symbolic act and yet goes on being used as an act of worship, then it is no longer real worship.

The importance of the idea that worship is a symbolic act vis à vis the process of secularization is twofold.

First, it shows that the process of secularization is constitutively ambivalent, i.e. has a double edge. For, secularization ultimately implies a change in the fundamental human—i.e. religious—symbols. On the one hand, it destroys forms of worship, on the other, it purifies worship. If everybody at a given time in a given culture had the same symbolic exponent or exponential factor, secularization could be seen as the healthy metabolic process by which a certain society got rid of obsolete cultic forms in order to acquire new ones. But the fact is that society does not present this homogeneity and consequently what appears to some as the liberating process of a healthy demythologization seems to others the most insidious example of the forces of evil undermining the right order of things. Perhaps tolerance, which is the sociological translation of the word patience, could here acquire a very special relevance.

The ambivalence is all the more visible if we consider the double dynamism of the present-day world: on the one hand there is undoubtedly a process of universalization and even uniformation. This re-inforces the challenge to find a genuinely universal and really human form of worship. Contemporary man abhors nothing more than esoterism and closed groups. On the other hand, there is also a parallel trend towards the particular and the concrete; the human being wants to express himself and this is only possible within a particular context and against a definite background. The liturgy here meets the challenge of having to be concrete and meaningful for a particular group while allowing forms of expression which have relevance only in a very special context.

Second, the idea of worship as a symbolic act also explains the persistence of worship even when it is no longer an expression of the belief of the individual. Because worship is a symbolic act and the symbols have a peculiar consistency of their own, because of the symbolic aspect of reality, the fact that a certain act is not found meaningful by a particular individual does not mean that it is incapable of conveying or carrying that symbolic reality which is no longer experienced by this particular individual. In other words, the power of ritual expressions is so great, the thrust of symbolic actions so powerful that sometimes these very actions are of themselves capable of conveying their message to future generations. The mechanical though faithful repetition of a certain ritual by some scrupulous priestly class has, for instance, often been the sole means of preserving a fundamental rite. One may recall, for example the fidelity to the Roman Catholic Liturgy during the XVIII century or the conservatism of some priestly castes in India. Though hardly anybody performed the symbolic, cultic acts with that minimal degree of consciousness that we would today consider necessary to save them from being called mere superstitions, this was nevertheless the 'providential' way in which both the Christian and the Vedic sacrifices were preserved.

We must thus beware of over-hurried and sweeping

iconoclastic furies. The subject of worship is not merely an individual or even a particular generation or group. Symbolical actions have a peculiar value of their own, for without being utterly independent of the human being (otherwise we would have sheer magic), they are also not totally dependent on a particular group of persons. The balance is a delicate and difficult one.

We have already made allusion to the difference between a sign and a symbol. Whereas the former is an epistemic device pointing to the 'thing', the relationship between the symbol and the symbolized reality is a *sui generis* one. The symbol is neither a substitute for the 'thing' nor the 'thing in itself', but the thing as it appears, as it expresses itself, as it manifests itself. This manifestation, however, is not the manifestation of some attribute or some effect of the 'thing' but the primordial manifestation, the genuine epiphany of the thing, so that outside or beyond that manifestation there is nothing except a mental hypothesis. I am a symbol of myself and, understanding this phrase not as an objective but sub-jective, genitive, we could add that I am the symbol of that self which only in the symbol *is* and manifests itself. Being, one could generalize, is the symbol of it-self, like the person is the symbol of the I. I 'am' not my body or my face, but my body and my face are symbols of myself, of a self which outside the body and its face has no being and is thus nothing. I cannot identify myself with my symbol but nor can I separate myself from it. I exist only in my symbol. In this sense I am my symbol (I am my body, etc.).

Using the accepted terminology of a transcendental difference or ontological difference (which Heidegger would call *transzendenhaft* as opposed to *transzendental*) as that difference between beings along with their entity and Being; remembering the transcendent or theological difference between God and beings, we would like to introduce the *symbolic difference* as that existing between the symbol and the reality, i.e., that peculiar difference between the reality (which is, only in so far as it is in its symbol) and its symbol. This difference is neither epistemic nor ontological—it is 'symbolical'. We cannot catch any being if we do not grasp its symbol, or rather if we do not discover the symbol of that reality which discloses itself only in its own and proper symbol. There 'is' no reality independent of its proper symbol. There is no symbol if it is not the symbol of a reality. But the reality does not lie 'behind' or 'beyond', but discloses itself only as symbol. In point of fact what the reality *is*, is its symbol; the *is* is the symbol of the real.

It will appear from what has been said that the criterion for discriminating between an authentic and a non-authentic form of worship cannot be the individualistic reaction: 'Is it actually meaningful to me?' It could still be very meaningful to others either to my contemporaries or perhaps to people of later generations. Indeed, if an act is not saying anything to me I may be allowed and perhaps I shall even have the duty not to perform it. I personally may find it repugnant to go on murmuring *Kyrie eleison,* but that in itself does not justify my condemning this repeated plea for mercy as nothing but hocus-pocus or as a remnant of the obscurantism of past ages.

But if this is the case, are we not justifying the dragging on for ever of obsolete forms of worship? Certainly not. Cultures and also cults, like human beings, are all mortal and we have to provide for a normal metabolism. On the other hand, merely to apply democratic techniques in this area in order to decide what should be kept or modified would amount to a denial not only of every religious tradition, indeed of the reality of tradition itself, but also of the very nature of worship, which is a free personal act and not merely a collective submission to the majority for the sake of the pragmatic functioning of a community.

We confront here an inescapable challenge to every belief and to every religion (sacred or secular): the existence of the other pole, the other shore, the trans-, super-, or extra-human factor. Whatever it may be called—God, Nothingness, Humanity, Future . . . there exists always another agency which transcends the purely individual, and which by definition provides the ultimate criterion.

Now, how are we to know that which traditionally has been called the Will of God? Here emerges the proper *locus* of the Church as the agency with authority to decide what is a genuine expression of a belief and what is not. However, I cannot now enter into this point but, in order to avoid misunderstanding, would only add that the Church that emerges here as the sole agency capable of solving the dilemma can neither be equated with any human authority, nor with any quasi-magical or anthro-pomorphically conceived supra-human device. Again, the theandric aspect of reality here emerges. But, only a brief allusion to this will be made in the next section, for we must restrict ourselves to our problem.

It remains here for us to sum up the rationale behind these methodological remarks.

In order to find the place of worship in a secular age we cannot adopt a merely pragmatic attitude and experiment to see if it 'works'. We have to inquire into the very nature of worship. In this way we discover that worship is the expression of a belief and we deduce, accordingly, that different types of worship will stand for different types of belief.

Taking into account all the words of caution uttered

and the provisos made, we have also come to the conclusion that unless we are prepared to fall into an irrational position, the forms of worship cannot shun philosophical analysis. Philosophy or, if we prefer, theology, has its say in screening acts of worship and analysing their assumptions. Thus they may discover forms which no longer symbolize that for which they stand. They may say, for instance, that the assumptions underlying big, penitential processions, which were once convened to bear witness to the fear of God's wrath, that is a God who could only be appeased by the blood and suffering of his worshippers, are no longer tenable for they no longer reflect our understanding of the Divine. The conclusion would then have to be drawn that such forms of worship were a distortion of faith rather than an expression of belief.

But we have come also to the conclusion that a purely rational and theoretical approach, though necessary to reject spurious forms, is not sufficient to create or to inspire positive forms of worship. For this, another factor is needed, a factor which constitutes the third section of this methodological chapter.

3. FAITH IN THE SPIRIT

Not even methodologically can we equate life with reflection or the living expression of a belief with a rational, or sometimes merely a reasonable, manifestation of it.

The theological criterion is necessary but not sufficient. A human concern about the role and place of worship in our times, cannot be reduced to deductive theological theorems or merely to deep philosophical insights. The living problem of worship cannot be decided, and much less prescribed, by philosophers,

theologians or academicians; it does not belong primarily
to the theoretical level.

Recently I remember finding myself explaining to
three learned theologians, experts in liturgical matters,
and at the same time highly spiritual men—of more than
one Christian persuasion, incidentally—some forms of
worship performed by a small group of Christians 7,000
kilometres away and spiritually equally distant from the
world of my three friends. While listening to my own
description I could not but share in the concern and think
the same cautions and provisos which my listeners
eventually put forward. All were men of experience and
imagination, but my endeavour to describe, while sitting
in a 'trattoria' of the Trastevere, the efforts involved in
expressing and living the Christian mystery on the shores
of the Ganges was bound to be a failure. I am not saying
that the churchmen were not right. I am only pointing out
that their comments, valuable as they were could not be
the decisive and positive element, nor the inspiring
force in expressing Christian belief and shaping liturgy.

What I am trying to suggest is that the *locus theo-
logicus* for our problem is neither Academia, nor Vatic-
anum (neither Philosophy, nor Theology) but the concrete Assembly in a particular spot, the voice of the
Spirit, life amid the bustle of the street, or in the solitude
of one's own room, the house, or—why not?—the studio
of the artist and also of the theologian!

How has any liturgy come about? We see examples of
how every day. Not by decree or by mere thought and
decision, but by the will of the community, by an
upsurge of the Spirit, by a force of circumstances, by an
act of inspired creation, by the spontaneity of a situation.
We can only provide a 'frame' in which the Spirit can
thrive but in which shallowness, base instincts and
irrational forces will not prevail.

24

Now, how are we to make room for the Spirit? Is not this intention by very definition, contradictory? If understood in a narrow sense, yes, indeed. Who am I to provide a situation in which the Spirit may act? Freedom is not something which can be decided upon or manipulated in advance. But our mood can be expectant, humble and full of acceptance and our attitude towards our time and towards our generations can be one of confidence. I say generations because one is already declining and another is pushing strongly from behind. We can cultivate an attitude of sympathy not only for the young, but also for the old. We can, in brief, try to liberate our mind from its own boundaries and simply try to experience what the foolishness of the Cross and madness of wisdom may mean. Both the scope and quality of our belief can improve and we can approach this problem with that humility which knows that all we can do is to hope along the way and to love during the investigation.

Worship, then, is not only following a way, but creating one, not only looking back to the past, but 'piercing' into the future, or, in other words, it is not only the function of the priest, but the task of the prophet.

One word more regarding the prophetic vocation. It is not fitting for a prophet to die outside his spiritual home, nor to die at the hands of any but his own people. It is the mark of a prophet that he is ready to lay down his life for his brethren and not run away. This sacrifice is made because the preservation of his life is not of ultimate importance to him. The prophet is the man—or the woman, of course—who does not step outside and leave the Church (or whatever community it may be) in order to avoid contamination by the sins of his brethren. He does not keep quiet either, for the sake of a false peace.

He knows that his life is his only power, and he puts it at stake constantly. By the simple law of probabilities, if he goes on raising his voice and risking his life, he is finally going to strike the right note and then be put to a violent, or perhaps peaceful, death.

I am not extolling the prophet at the expense of the community. I am only trying to suggest that this is a feature inherent in the nature of things. It belongs to the Church—a term which I shall not specify further—to offer resistance to change, to put innovations to the test but also to allow the prophet to perform his function. Only in the struggle unto death between the priest and the prophet is the life of the Church possible. Her very existence, moreover is due to a constant and ever renewed sacrifice. The cry of our time is for fair play, but both the priest and the prophet are fully conscious that the fight is unto death. It is out of this death that life rises again. Let us not forget this. In the case of worship we have a living, shining example before us. The prophet cannot decide what is right, nor can he attempt to build an exclusively prophetic Church (it would only defeat his own purpose) but he has to go on with his non-conformist or revolutionary vocation. The priest, for his part, should not condemn, nor can he stop tradition or choke life (it would undermine his own right of existence) but he has to maintain loyalty to the structures and fidelity to the past. The Church is the place of sacrifice and this sacrifice of priest and prophet is also liturgy. Worship is not only a sentimental song; it is the life of the Church and humanity.

Worship is life and life cannot be dictated or called into existence by law. There is but one constant and universal feature of every life; it is fostered and maintained by death. Life goes on, because there is a constant process of death and new life. The letter killeth. The point is not to avoid death or preserve what we imagine to be still alive, but out of death to make room for resurrection.

We have so far said that any purely rational criterion *a posteriori* is not sufficient in order to find the right place of worship and the ways of worship at a given time. We have further said that the rational criteria which we may find *a priori* are certainly necessary, because reason always has the veto power, as it were, to discard as not worthy of human dignity anything which transgresses the right exigencies of reason; but it is one thing to recognize this negative role of reason, and another to pull all of our lives in the hands of reason, when we are, even by reason alone, capable of discovering that reason has its limits and cannot justify itself. It is here that we still find the lack of a sufficient criterion and we are bound to say that if we take life in its totality and the existential situation of mankind realistically we have to recognize that we have not the tools to handle intellectually any existential situation. There is always room for another possible reality which will define itself and justify itself once it has appeared and made itself real. We may agree that we should not stifle the Spirit, but it still remains true that the Spirit blows where it wills.

Chapter 2
SECULARIZATION

Philosophical Reflections

So much has been said and written, especially recently, about the Sacred and the Profane, that it is only with the greatest of caution that I now attempt to sum up the present-day controversy by suggesting the application of three concepts, which may help to render a little more intelligible this complex affair.

The history of mankind as well as the history of human consciousness individually and collectively, i.e. from the point of view of its personal development, could be conveniently understood and heuristically expounded under the three headings of heteronomy, autonomy and ontonomy.

By heteronomy we understand a world view, as well as an anthropological degree of consciousness, which relies on a hierarchical structure of reality, which considers that the regulations in any sphere of being come from a higher instance, and are in each case responsible, so to speak, for the proper functioning of that particular being or sphere of being.

By autonomy we understand the world as well as the human being to be *sui iuris*, i.e. self-determined and determinable, each being a law unto its self. This autonomy means that any injunction from outside, even if it is said to come from above, is regarded as an abusive imposition.

By ontonomy we mean that degree of awareness, which, having overcome the individualistic attitude as well as the monolithic view of reality, regards the whole universe as unity so that the regulation of a particular being is neither self-imposed nor dictated from above, but a part of the whole discovering or following its destiny. Ontonomy is the realisation of the *nomos*, the law of the *on*, being, at that profound level where unity does not impinge upon diversity, but where the latter is rather the unique and proper manifestation of the former. It rests on the *specular* character of reality, in which each 'part' mirrors the whole in a way proper to it.

Each of these three world-views have developed through the ages valid intuitions and it would be an anachronism as well as a methodological error to judge one period with the degree of consciousness attained by another. We have called them 'kairological' moments in the history of religions as well as in the history of mankind and the development of human consciousness. They are, in fact, not only *or even mainly* three periods in the history of culture, but three fundamental religious and human attitudes corresponding to three anthropological degrees of consciousness. They do not succeed one another in chronological order, but acquire kairological momentum according to the internal or external development of a concrete situation. We are thus not forcing facts into a foreign, *a priori* scheme, but trying to understand the facts, discovering in them their heteronomic, autonomic or ontonomic relationship to the rest of reality. In what follows we shall not waste time in pushing this working hypothesis too far. For our purpose it will suffice to consider the main insights which these three human and historical attitudes have developed regarding our specific problem. It should not be necessary to stress that we are going to emphasize only the positive aspects of these three moments, leaving aside those all too obvious abuses degradations and exaggerations which occur once these values no longer correspond to the degree of awareness that the common man has of himself and reality.

1. SACRED HETERONOMY

Worship has traditionally been linked with the realm of the sacred, the realm in which relationship with the transcendental was said to take place. The sacred was judged to be superior to the profane and to possess a certain power over it, so that in a sense the profane has had to justify its existence by proving its service to the sacred: 'Quid hoc ad aeternitatem?' This relationship was traditionally considered to be one of heteronomy: God is not only superior to man but also his creator and thus his lord. Man has not only to obey God, but also the hierarchical order; the religious head is not only superior to the political one (Pope to Emperor, priest to official, brahmin to *kṣatrya*, Church to State) but also gives laws to the latter; spiritual values are not only higher than material ones, but they fix the boundaries in which the latter may develop; Theology is the master of mere Philosophy and then Philosophy determines almost *a priori* the fields of and the rules for scientific investigation. As we know this 'Weltanschauung' is still to some extent part of our modern outlook. From the point of view of heteronomy the rules and laws which determine the development of an inferior sphere of being are provided by the higher sphere. It is a hierarchical conception of the world. Not only cesaropapism and theocracy, but also the caste system and state-communism could be adduced as examples of a cancerous heteronomy.

The traditional notion of worship has been determined

by this world-view. Worship is the highest action man can perform on earth. Everything else has to be directed so as to facilitate a life of worship. Is not worship the 'loving' reverence paid to the highest instance—which is always right? The brahmin and the priest have the highest rank in such a society. On the other hand, worship has no need to invade every realm. It has the highest position, it towers over the rest of human activities, but must delegate to them other pursuits of human life. The brahmin has to be poor, the clergy detached. Worship has a sphere of its own: the sacred, which is precisely that which is severed from what is not sacred: the *pro-fanum*. The holy is the *sanctum*, that which is segregated from the world.

The rules for the development of the liturgy in such a society are obviously going to be different from the rules in a secular society and thus the reform of the liturgy in a hierarchical society will differ markedly from the patterns of development found in a predominantly secular society.

In a heteronomic conception of the world there would seem to be three operative values regarding our problem of worship. On the anthropological level *adoration* is the key word, on the metaphysical level *eternity* is the dominant concept and on the cosmological level *sacrifice* is the dominating and ever-recurrent category. A brief sketch will here suffice.

Adoration means that attitude in which the human being simply surrenders to a divine power. This total surrender being regarded as a positive act by which the worshipper far from losing anything actually realises himself.

The world in which adoration is possible is a heteromic world and its meaningfulness rests on the triple assumption (a) of an ego which is utterly dependent,

31

contingent, zero and eventually sinful; (b) that there is an absolute in a personified form, a God who is pure goodness; (c) that salvation or the goal of the human being is connected with the recognition of a) and b). In other words, the spirituality of adoration tries to combine in a peculiar way the three classical methods of most traditional spiritualities: the *karma*, the *jñana* and the *bhakti* yogas. In order really to practice worship, in the sense of adoration, one has to be, in fact, an ascetic who recognizes that there is much to purify and much to get rid of in human nature, that man as such has no worth in or from himself, that humility is an ontological and not merely a moral virtue. One has, further, to be a kind of mystic, i.e., a man who has really discovered that God alone is the real and everlasting reality, the total Being, the Perfect One, immanent and transcendent reality at the same time; one has to be overwhelmed by the sense of God, not as a mighty power or primordial cause, but rather, as an all-pervading presence, a caring providence and an absolute person: these are all attributes of the Godhead, which only if personally realized can lead to the third feature of an act of adoration: love. In point of fact only love enables us to perform and to understand an act of adoration. This explains the language of man in adoration: 'He is the Lord, to whom all honour and glory alone belong, he can do with us as he pleases, we are his slaves, servants, sons, toys, zeros, etc.: his sovereign claim over us gives us life and happiness, because we have experienced that to serve him is to reign, that to recognize his lordship is to be free, that there is ultimately no place for two, that to be lost in the beloved is to be one with him and this is what we really are meant to be and indeed what we long to be.'

The second operative value in worship is the meta-physical assumption of the reality of *eternity* as a heterogeneous reality to time. Eternity has a proper consistency, so to speak, which makes it totally independent of time. Eternity is neither infinite time nor a kind of supra-or, for that matter, infra-temporal reality, but totally incomparable and incommensurable reality, forming no relation whatsoever with temporal reality. In order to be, the human being has to transcend time; the word for this is eternity. It is the specific character of divinity. This is not, properly speaking, a dualistic conception of the universe, though it has only too often given that impression. Both a certain type of Hindu Vedânta and a certain form of Christian scholasticism could be adduced as examples of the metaphysical assumption that God and the world are not in relationship. Adoration only makes sense as the total holocaust of creatureliness if there is eternity ready to receive with open arms the absolute surrender of the creature. Adoration is not a suicidal act, though it may look like this to the outsider, precisely because he does not see the reality of the other shore, which cannot be expressed in any of the terms at the disposal of the creature. Eternity is the term for this unutterable and unthinkable reality. About its consistency or ontological status the different theological and metaphysical schools are obviously in disagreement nor are they able to agree on whether the term eternity is the most appropriate choice. But all agree that temporal reality has to be transcended.

The third operative value we want to consider is the cosmological conception of *sacrifice*, as it was essentially understood by almost all the world's religious traditions before the autonomous influence somewhat devalued the concept. The proper domain of sacrifice is *orthopraxy*, the domain of the ontologically full action, the sacred action, the action which is not empty of content, the action which in fact produces and brings salvation, in whatever form the latter may be understood. The business of man on earth is to achieve happiness, to attain salvation, to reach the goal, however one may choose to describe it. But how is one to achieve a peaceful, or a justified or a fulfilled life? The acts by which one creates such a life or reaches such a goal are sacrificial, re-enactments of the primordial act by which the world, man and even time, came into being. The sacrifice is by its nature a theandric act, an act in which God and man have to work together in order that the world be maintained; it is a cosmic act, for the subsistence of the world depends upon it. God alone cannot perform the sacrifice, he requires human co-operation; man alone is impotent to sacrifice, let alone to make the sacrifice acceptable, he requires divine help, divine grace.

With these main conceptions as operating values worship appears to be that act by which man works out his salvation. For this he must adore God and throw himself into the domain of God's sovereign love, living a life which corresponds to the saving sacrifice which he performs according to the different traditional patterns. Any act of worship will express in one way or other these three fundamental values and be geared to their cultivation. If we examine any of the long-standing forms of religious worship we find that they have practically the same structure.

The image of God in heteronomy is rather non-personified and more like the absolute Being. Access to it is by *jñāna*, by *gnosis*, rather than by any other means. Here, mysticism comes into its own.

2. PROFANE AUTONOMY

As a reaction against such a world-view we have the almost opposite notion of autonomy. As opposed to the

Empire we get the Republic; rather than the Church, the State; rather than Philosophy, Science; rather than the Sacred, the Profane. Each sphere of being has its own rules and no interference is tolerated: the nations are sovereign, reason is the ultimate arbiter, no individual has a higher authority than another and only a democratic procedure pragmatically accepted can introduce some practical principle of order. Science, as a whole and in its various parts, regulates its own business in which nobody may interfere, for investigation is free and science sovereign; the sacred may still be valid, but in its proper corner; religion is a private affair and has no privilege whatsoever; it regulates a part of human activity for those who still believe in it, but that is all; it is a part and not the whole. The minister of religion is a citizen like any other; religion can be taught in school, like any other subject, with the proviso that it has to be absolutely optional: for religion, unlike objective science, is essentially sectarian, limited. It has cost centuries of struggle and evolution to vindicate the rights of the so-called inferior spheres of being and now each of them claims its own independence.

We know this picture so well that there is no need for further description. It suffices to say that the highest concession that such a world-view can tolerate is to recognise that religion and religious values have a certain right to existence and so of allowing such forms of worship as do not interfere with those values that are really universal and thus important for the well-being of a society.

Autonomy is in the last analysis always a reaction against heteronomy; it is almost invariably a rebellion against the abuses of the heteronomic structure. As opposed to the three key values of the former period, here the operative words are *respect* or reverence, *temporality,* and *service* or work.

From the autonomic point of view, heteronomic adoration appears to be either idolatry because the worshipper seems to mistake the concept (or the image) of God for the God himself, or as sheer superstition because genuine adoration amounts to an inhuman surrender of the personality and an abdication of human rights it thus leads to a total degradation of man, making him believe that he is just an instrument, a dead thing in the hands of an almighty power.

Instead of the ecstatic attitude of the worshipper in adoration a more autonomic spirituality will stress the *reverence* and *respect* due to God, emphasizing that God is not an absolute tyrant and that even He is bound by his own law, so that He cannot transgress the boundaries of what is good and true or even beautiful. Autonomy is that anthropological attitude which does not allow for pure ecstatic postures. On the contrary, it is proud of its discovery of self-awareness and of its critical attitude. There is still place for God, but for a God who respects the rules of the game, for a God, as it were, whose nature and whose attributes I discover and in a sense I postulate. There is little place for mysticism here. The mystic approach is always somehow outside the normal pattern, always transcending the given structures, an approach for which there is little justification in the autonomous world. It is not by chance that mysticism is always suspect in an autonomous world-view.

The attitude of reverence presupposes a self-critical awareness of the worshipper's own position, the subject who worships enters also into the picture. Reverence certainly implies, as etymology itself substantiates, a standing in awe and almost fear: *re-vereri.*

Akin to reverence is *respect* and in point of fact, this is really the category within autonomy for reverence is of a more transitional nature. Reverence is due to God, but the more conscious worship of autonomy will first stress that this reverence is tinged with respect and secondly that it flows into respect, i.e., esteem and veneration which extends also to all men.

Respect no longer implies the cloistered, i.e. closed and ineffable, inaccessible God; it no longer stands for an apophatic attitude, but, as its etymology suggests, implies vision and investigation: it has 'regard' for the thing respected, precisely because it 'sees' its value, beauty and truth. *Respectus,* comes from *respicere,* 'to look', and is connected with the root *spec,* from which also come *speciosus* and *species,* with all the shades of meaning from 'beauty' to 'appearance'. Respect is surely democratic, it shows esteem and honour because it looks at the value of the object so respected; it has 'regard' and finds it 're-markable', it 'marks', notices, sees the value of it. It is no longer sheer surrender, conditionless obedience. It is ready to obey when it sees the reasons why it has to obey—though, strictly speaking, one does not need to see the reasonableness of any given commandment.

Worship is here reverence for God, but also something more, respect for Him, for his plans, for the world, his creation and for men his creatures. It is not ecstatic and has little place for dance, but it underscores reading, pondering, knowing. The worshipper, here, does not intend to lose himself, but rather re-gain something, it is an act of self-realization. It is not surrender to, but recognition of God's Power, Providence or whatever we may like to call it. The image of God is here eminently personified; theism is now the rule as opposed to the more metaphysical Being of the heteronomic position.

Personal relationships are here basic. *Bhakti* in the sense of personal love is here the norm.

Temporality is the metaphysical element of this attitude. The value here is no longer eternity, but that specific form of human time which we may call temporality. Temporality is neither eternity, which belongs to God alone and has no relationship whatsoever with time, nor is it indiscriminate time which is a mere succession of events. The human time here called temporality is a peculiar mode of existence, of gathering human existence together, of accumulating the past into the present, of carrying the past in the present and stretching toward the future. Temporality is a quality more than a quantity, it is a qualitative accumulation, i.e., a heaping up of the past stored, like an accumulator, in the present, giving us strength to shape, i.e. to live the future. Temporality is not just time, so that it is not irrelevant whether you die young or old. The ontological growth is temporal development. Not to waste one's time or the time of the others is of the utmost importance. Autonomy is proud of its discovery of the value of temporality and of its distinction from mere time. Temporality is historicity and memory.

We could perhaps draw the following table for the sake of expediency:

temporicity
{
eviternity *(angels)*. Only future

temporality *(men)*. Present and future

time *(physical things)* Past, present and future.
}

Temporicity would be the generic mode of duration of beings, the mode of being in the world, the quality of their existence, of their subsistence, the way in which beings are: it is not something external to them, but a dimension of their being, a quality of their own being: that by which they 'go on' be-ing. Man's temporicity, that we have called temporality, has in a sense no past, the past is in a way (the specifically human way) present: we are our own past, the past is integrated in us, is not 'past' but present and effective. To say 'Thou shall be with me today in paradise' is not an act of mercy or an injustice vis à vis those who have not the chance to 'hear' for themselves such words, but it is an expression that we carry all along with us and always all our past so that my today sums up, contains all that I am.

Temporality is thus not an object nor a 'thing in itself'; it is rather a manner, the proper temporal and human manner in which man ek-sists, perdures, endures, stretches his be-ing. Temporality is not a frozen pattern either, it is not a recipient but the net in which men are. If temporality disappears men also cease to exist. This is the great achievement of autonomy: temporality is real, is not merely a passing and intermediate stage between non-being and eternity, it is not a provisional set up for the 'time-being', not merely a stepping stone to be left behind. To look back for the past is an anachronism and, what is more, barren. In the autonomic world-view a certain type of conservativism or traditionalism is looked down upon as a blind mistake.

No need to stress the ambiguity of all such insights. They can be considered most destructive or most purifying; they can appear as destroying any sense of transcendence or as a coming of age and taking seriously the human condition blurred by heteronomic superimpositions.

Worship here is not to kill time or to sacrifice creatureliness, nor to do what otherwise is not done (all typical heteronomic features) but to use time, to profit by it, to shape it and form it. Hence, the third value mentioned above.

The cosmological assumption of this world-view lies in the fact that the world is so made that we have to work on it in order to collaborate in its maintenance. This is also known to the heteronomic attitude, but the approach is radically different. Here it is a real 'human' work whereas there is a collaboration in a theandric activity. Each sphere of being is here supposed to be able and capable of sustaining itself by its own effort. It is no longer the king or the father or for that matter God, who looks after his subjects, children or creatures, but a democratic mind makes everybody responsible for his own subsistence to the extent that the sociological 'liberal' pattern evaluates a person according to his work and his work according to its usefulness, it also denies the right of existence to those who refuse to 'work'.

Here liturgy becomes work, the *ergon* of the *laos*, the work of the people; work which has to be unselfish and thus provide a service for others, help for those who cannot work, uplift for the less gifted, the less developed and the less able. Reverence and respect lead to work and service. Everybody has to work, has to serve, has to collaborate for the maintenance of society and the world at large.

In the autonomic world a worship of mere praise, of pure interiorization would be considered the highest betrayal; a mockery of human dignity and a falling back into the obscurantism of an age in which man was not fully mature.

The anthropological insight of autonomy is clear. Man realises himself not by seeing, knowing, contemplating, not by a passive acceptance of reality, not by merely loving what comes to him, but by doing, acting and shaping something outside himself, by projecting himself into a scheme, a plan, a role. He has to make himself and make himself useful. A great part of psychotherapy and psychoanalysis is devoted to saving man from his unassimilated introversion, or recoiled interiority (privacy, narcissism and fear). It throws him into a world, not only to redeem him but also to serve that world, man, thus, comes to believe that he occupies a meaningful place in the universe and plays a vital role in society.

The shift is clear. The emphasis is not on religion as previously conceived, but on Science, Reason and Society. The profane here replaces the sacred. Worship is no longer a way of mastering the Unknown or the Mysterious, of placating divine wrath, asking for divine mercy or praising a super-human love, but the recognition of our dignity and our role of collaborating with the whole world to bring about a better life here on earth. This is the case even if some still believe that there is something reserved for them in the hereafter. Worship, in a scientific age must have recourse to psychology, music, art and indeed anything likely to give the individual the confidence, the faith and the love he needs for a full human existence. If God helps, he is not altogether banished, but he is certainly conditioned. He has to accept the rules of the game if he is to be allowed into the picture.

3. THEANDRIC ONTONOMY

This neologism stands for the recognition neither of heteronomy, i.e. the regulation of the activity of a particular being by laws proceeding from another higher being, nor of autonomy, i.e. the affirmation that each field is absolutely self-normative and patron of its own destiny. Ontonomy is intended to express the recognition of the inner regularities of each field of activity or sphere of being in the light of the whole. The whole is, in fact, neither different from nor merely identical with any one field or sphere. Ontonomy rests on the assumption that the universe is a whole, that there is an internal and constitutive relationship between all and every part of reality, that nothing is disconnected and that the development and progress of one being is not to be at the expense of another—not because it should or ought not, but for the same reason adduced in the case of cancer, namely that neither promotes the life of the whole organism nor is of any utility for the affected organ.

In our case ontonomy does not accept any dualism or metaphysical dichotomy: the field of the sacred is no longer defined in opposition to that of the secular, nor is a development of worship made at the cost of work, politics or any other human activity.

I may add without wishing to be polemic or discriminatory, that if the Christian message stands for anything it is for this experience of the theandric reality of every being, of which the revelation in Jesus Christ, real man and real God is the paradigm. In Christ there is not the Man on the one hand and God on the other; neither of these two intrinsically united dimensions has the upper hand, so that it has no meaning to say that Christ is more godly than human or vice-versa. The veil of separation is torn to pieces and the integration of reality begins with the redemption of man. Perhaps this idea of re-integration seen in the light of redemption may eventually influence the reform of the patterns of worship in our own day.

Parallel to the previous descriptions, here too we can see three main values: *devotion* or love as the anthropological assumption, *tempiternity* as the metaphysical basis and *participation* or mysticism as the cosmological foundation of the ontonomic world-view. To be sure, if ontonomy does not want to be another 'view', but a certain synthesis and harmonic, higher unity between the two previous attitudes, the emphasis on these three values must not be one of exclusivism, but of inclusivism with regard to the other positions.

The fundamental trend of the human being in this connection is seen in love or devotion. This latter concept is understood, according to its etymological suggestion, as a profound dedication, a personal conse-cration and earnest attachment to a cause, an ideal or a person. But not as a blind trend. On the contrary it is not only a 'vow' (*devotus* comes from *devovere*) but also a speech, a proclamation, a logos (*dedicatio* comes from *dedicare*, which is a variation on *dicere*: to proclaim, to speak).

Love is here not understood in opposition to know-ledge, but as an integration of the centrifugal and the centripetal dynamism of man, as a movement certainly outside and above myself, which can well be ecstatic, but also as a movement from outside toward my innermost centre, as a recognition of the greatness of my aim, which I would not have been able to detect were it not for the love impelling me already in that direction. It is not a vicious but a vital circle, as human experience proves almost every day on all levels. Once on the way we discover the values of the way and the way itself. And it 'was' because of this (pre)discovery that we set ourselves upon the way.

The implication of this ordinary and almost universal experience is that the human being finds or rather creates its value in fulfilling itself, i.e. in recognising and believing in his own value and acting accordingly. In other words, there are neither merely objective values independent of the human being, nor are there merely subjective values dependent on him. The relationship is constitutive; the human person is a part of the whole in such a way that his 'personal' and subjective ideas, convictions, and actions are an integral part of the objective world. The objective *is* in so far as it is subjective, assimilated, personal, seen to be such, incarnated, really subjectivized. The subjective, on the other hand, *is* in so far as it is objective and even objectified, realized, set in motion, crystallized, made practical and put into practice. The relationship of God, Man, Cosmos is not the relationship of three objects (or two, for that matter, if we coalesce Man and Cosmos into the abstract notion of creature), not of three subjects, nor of that of one Supreme Subject with one or two objects. The relationship cannot be dealt with by either the parameters of the heteronomy or those of the autonomy. There is no God independent of Man (except in a very peculiar and abstract thinking, which begins by abstracting from reality) nor is Man independent of God and the same applies to the world.

The consequence of this (which we cannot develop here conveniently) is that whatever man does without his internal participation and internal conviction or subjective involvement is not only not licit or wrong, but also *is not*, has no objective reality. Love cannot be commanded. It would simply be not love. Nor can faith be imposed, for that matter. And conversely, whatever a man does without a real participation, whatever claims to be subjective without an objective involvement is simply not real. It is not. Dedication cannot be the fruit of a mere intellectual awareness or of a decision of the will. The ontonomic anthropology overcomes the object -subject split not only in epistemology but also in ontology and certainly in anthropology.

Tempiternity, we said, is the operative work in the ontonomic attitude. Tempiternity, as its very name would like to suggest, is neither eternity (an objectified notion belonging exclusively to God), nor temporality (a much too subjective concept and the monopoly of the human being).

If we had to complete the table given above we would offer the following scheme,

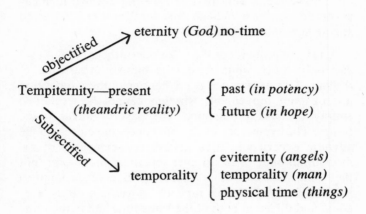

The fundamental intuition of tempiternity flows from the experience of the present in all its depth, discovering in it not only the past in potency and the future in hope but also what the objectified projection of mankind has called eternity and the subjectified human sensibility has called time (or temporality in our terms). The experience of the present, in fact, pierces, as it were the crust of the provisional and the flowing, not to fall onto a static intemporal bed, not to deny time, but to relish its kernel, so to speak. Any profound human experience occurs in time and yet is not bound to or by time. It has no meaning to fix a mystical experience temporally, it is senseless to say 'I love you for five minutes', it is incongruous to affirm that death is not real because it abolishes subjective time, it is incoherent to relate what is intrinsically an aesthetic experience to any time outside its own temporality, it is impossible to have any experience of time during an intellectual discovery, in that 'moment' in which we experience the small or great discovery of something which dawns on us for the first 'time', and so on. The very consciousness of time implies that man has a certain platform outside that kind of time, so as to enable him to be aware of it.

A very important corollary for our purpose, though we can only touch upon it, is the human experience of rhythm. This experience is neither one of mere repetition nor of pure movement. Rhythm cannot be explained simply because I remember the past or advance the future. The experience of rhythm comes the closest to the advaitic experience: it is neither consciousness of the monolithic one, or of an ever repetitive monotony, nor the consciousness of a dualistic diversity, or of a fundamentally different tune or movement. It is ever equal and different both at the same time and in the same place (be it the muscles of our limbs, the flashes in our eyes, or the sounds of our ears). It is a transtemporal experience, something which does not lead us away or distract from time but allows us to pierce through it, so that the kernel of time lays bare before us, as it were, or rather merges and becomes identified with us. In rhythm we express what otherwise could not be expressed or manifest; the expression is in and through time and yet the real symbol carried by the rhythm transcends time. Rhythm is a kind of liberation of time through time. And this applies in one way or another to any kind of rhythm, from the musical to the scientific, literary and cosmic rhythms.

Participation and in a certain way *mysticism* could be

the key words from a cosmological angle expressing the ontonomic experience.

The latter stands for the twofold conviction that (a) reality has a hidden and invisible dimension, which in one way or another can be brought to light or to the surface of the real, and that (b) only when one is aware or takes into account (even if in an unconscious way) this dimension of reality does an authentic human life emerge. By mysticism we may here understand that immediate contact with reality which causes the separation of subject-object to disappear as well as the distance implied in any kind of dualism.

The word participation is meant to convey that cosmological vision which sees the interdependence and interpenetration of all things and their mutual relationship as the deepest web of reality. According to this vision we *are* inasmuch as we participate in the whole and allow the whole to participate, i.e., to express itself in us. I am, inasmuch as the others are in me, inasmuch as I am involved in and committed to the whole of reality, inasmuch as I take part, i.e., I participate in the entire process of the universe.

To be a person does not mean to-be-there and remain isolated or disconnected from the whole. The person does not have an existence of his own, he is insofar as he participates, i.e. is a part and a conscious part that is performing a certain and unique *function*. In order to perform this role, we need a mask, because what we are, as parts, is this mask (there is nothing else behind or beyond—and yet that nothingness sustains the mask, and lets it play its role). We are persons, i.e. functions, operating centres of a bundle of relationships.

Worship here means that act by which we express in one way or another the fulness of the human person. It implies devotion, love, i.e. the heart, the emotions, as well as the dedication of our being and the consecration of our lives.

It implies, secondly, the integration of transtemporal reality and tempiternity as a fundamental dimension of the real. Worship is neither worldly nor other-worldly, but theandric; it implies an insight into the whole, an aspect of contemplation, the entire engagement of the mind, the mystic touch.

Thirdly, worship requires a participation in the cosmic process of the world, a share in the totalizing dynamism of reality, and in consequence an overcoming of individualism not only among men but also among things and in a very special way in God himself. Worship is participation in the whole of reality, it is a sacramental act in which matter and spirit, the divine and the human, the body and the mind, the angelic and the demonic, all collaborate in letting reality be by symbolizing itself in the symbol which reality is.

Within this context the answer to the question of why we should worship at all would run along the following lines: because otherwise I could neither be myself nor could you be yourself. The non-worshipful acts of my life are all lopsided; they do something for you, but there they stop. An act of worship is an act which allows and enables us to realize our being, to realize the cosmos, to be what really is. This is what the most practical experience attests every day when it says that you worship only when you are in a situation in which you can express really what you ultimately are without pretending in any sense, without being selfish or closed, or for that matter superficial and glib: and this is not always in solitude, not always in works, not always in fellowship, but at times includes all such moments. A thrill crosses you in worship; you are being geared again into the universe, and at the same time the universe is changing in and through you.

The image of God here is not so central; neither the theism of heteronomy nor the more deistic trends of autonomy are considered essential. It is by no means an atheistic nor an adeistic attitude, but it does not need to insist on the transcendent or on the immanent aspect of the godhead. *Jnāna* and *bhakti*, i.e. *gnosis* and *agape*, or in other words, knowledge and love, are here recognized and accepted, but these two elements are integrated in a *karmic* movement, i.e. in the dynamic of *orthopraxis*, which does not allow the subjective or the objective to gain the upper hand.

One may envisage the modern phenomenon of secularization according to any one of the three perspectives sketched above:

(a) Secularization will be, following the first scheme, the most blasphemous tearing asunder of the undefiled and seamless garment of a hierarchical and structured reality. It is the work of the Antichrist and the disrupture of all order; it is incompatible with any form of worship. Religion will have to resist the temptation of secularization, which amounts to sheer prostitution. One argument typical of this kind of approach is the pragmatic remark that all attempts at desacralising man recoil upon themselves: the sacred, which was expelled by the front-door, now enters through the back window: religious processions have been banned, but political parades take their place; sacred formalisms have been ridiculed but political paraphernalia are substituted for them. Sacramental life has been derided, but new sacraments in secular garb are introduced; veneration and worship have been branded as idolatry and superstition, but never as now have we had such examples of hero worship and of idols of all kinds. Religious authority has been undermined, as well as the divine origin of all authority, but never has the State had such powerful means of interference and domination as those made possible by the rebellious development of modern technology. We may think of the famous 'Jugendweihe' some years ago in East-Germany.

The tendency of the heteronomic attitude is clear and uncompromising: the lost order has to be restored, the errors have to be confessed, truly enough by both sides, but whereas 'we' have only made a wrong use of our power and sometimes perhaps abused our privileged situation, the error of the 'others' is substantial and fundamental. Moreover, only the restoration of the central role and traditional function of worship is going to permit man and society to undergo the regeneration which we are all seeking.

(b) The reaction of the autonomic attitude will be precisely the opposite of that described above. It will greet the secularization of man and society as the grand achievement of our times and the dethronement of the sacred as the greatest victory for the liberation of man, slave as he was under the dominion, if not the terror, of the sacred. This latter stood for the unknown; it constituted a pandering to the weakness and ignorance of man and simply served to instill in him resignation and passivity, thus blocking any progress and evolution.

According to this view, if worship is to have any meaning at all for the life of modern man, all its traditional forms must be relegated in a first period of transition to the private sector of human life so as to permit a subsequent enlightenment and a total liberation from such traditional forms of worship. Secondly, secular forms of worship must be found which are capable of expressing the core of worship in the very realm of the secular.

Within a Christian context, such an attitude will stress,

for instance, that the Eucharist has first of all, to be a meal that is not obscured by forms which distort not only its meaning and symbolism but its beauty and efficacity; it will stress that baptism or marriage are not magic acts and mysterious actions which bind men, but on the contrary, liberating experiences, which allow men to be more themselves; that prayer as an excuse in actions belonging to a forbidden sacred realm must be secularized and brought into the light of day. Autonomy will try to convert worship into work, meditation into an equally human action such as thinking and will try to find in the political life of man, not an overwhelming sense of awe or guilt because politics is not the real and ultimately important field of activity, but a 'pathos' which makes of them the most serious human activity, etc.

The tendency of the autonomic attitude is equally unmistakable: we have to get rid of sentimentalism and old attachments in order to be convinced that a new era is dawning upon man's consciousness, the era of radical secularism, which demands of the religious man a total conversion to the world and its values so as to be able to redeem them, in traditional parlance, or to enhance and to enrich them (to use modern and secular terminology). Real love of God is service to men and the most lofty religious service is not to sing the lauds of an invisible Creator, but to extol the possibilities of man himself so as to make possible a vital leap into the future and the true redemption of man from misery, malady, hatred and injustice.

I may have somewhat oversimplified these two attitudes, but I think I have expressed what is implied in them.

Whereas heteronomy would simply refuse to make any compromise, even going so far as to affirm that 'worship in a secular age' has more than ever to be the exalted sign

51

of the sacred, uncompromisingly upheld in contradiction to and confrontation with the modern world and its secular spirit, for only thus will it provide a unique lifebuoy to save mankind, once the present devastating wave of irreligion subsides. Whereas heteronomy, in fact, says that there is no worship of a secular world as such, autonomy emphatically affirms that the only meaningful and indeed possible worship in a secular age is none other than a secular, not to say secularized, worship. Worship itself has to undergo the purifying process through which history has gone if it wants to survive as something more than a museum piece in the dark and dusty chambers of the obscurantists.

(c) Ontonomy, on the other hand, will uphold neither an irreducible opposition between worship and secularization (the position of heteronomy), nor an identification which will make worship of secularized worship (the position of autonomy), but will consider worship to be one of the elements of secular life itself, making room for that very dimension of secularity which until now was not so termed and was either rejected as other-worldly or negated altogether. Ontonomy will make an effort to enlighten our vision so as to make us realize that the worship that matters is the worship *of* the secular world, but will interpret this genitive as a subjective genitive; it is the worship *of* (possessed by, coming from, corresponding and fitting to) this secular world.

The ontonomic attitude is, first of all, surely not a compromise, nor a kind of mediocre middle way avoiding the two extremes. It is an original position which is in a way, simpler than the other two attitudes both of which ultimately become dualistic. The ontonomic attitude begins by saying to the secularist, that nothing is more sacred than the secular while adding, for the traditionalist, that sacredness is not a value in itself, but a dimension of the one and only theandric reality.

The approach of this attitude will not be one of a simple restoration or thorough reform, but one which seeks to redeem all values, to use Christian terminology, without wanting to read into this any specifically Christian value. It will, for instance, transcend the dualistic or monistic scheme, both of which ultimately make worship either degrading or impossible. If, on the one hand, worship necessarily implies a Wholly Other, from all points of view bigger and better than I, we may easily throw on to him final responsibility for our own existence. If, on the other hand, it is assumed that there is only one monolithic reality, then there is no place for any authentic worship, this latter being relegated to sheer superstition. The ontonomic attitude, on the other hand, stressing the theandric nature of reality, discovers worship as precisely that conscious activity which transforms from within reality itself. But I shall refrain from putting forward here a whole theory of worship, my task being simply to clarify its relationship to secularization.

The ontonomic attitude will not regard the process of secularization as fundamentally evil; though it will not be blind to its dangers it will discover that there is an internal dynamism within any given human situation leading towards a deeper unity and that the only danger lies in schism, i.e., in the rupture of unity. Anthropologists tell us that at the beginning everything was sacred; we are now closing a circle by converting everything into the secular. The sacred and the profane are two aspects of one and the same thing and either is incomplete and even wrong the moment it wishes to have a separate, independent sphere of its own. First of all, they are correlative aspects, so that the sacred can only exist in contradistinction to the profane and vice versa. And secondly, they belong to a particular degree of consciousness of mankind, which is perhaps fading away today. To disentangle worship from the grip of either of them may be a task reserved for the coming generation; but we may manage to pave the way by building a bridge or discovering a bridle path connecting the sacred and the secular.

The process of secularization does not need to be envisaged as a mere reaction against the established sacred order, though in fact this may have been the case in the majority of instances. The distinction has been made between *secularization*, representing the progression from the sacred to the secular, *secularism*, as a secular order which may, in the event, still be tolerant of the sacred and its rights, and *secularity*, which would represent the intolerant destruction of any sacred order. Whatever the immediate causes of secularization may have been and however this secularization may have taken place (these are certainly two most important questions,) the whole secular outlook on reality does not need to be considered exclusively from the autonomic point of view, i.e. as reaction or rebellion and as totally incompatible with a deep religiousness and thus with an authentic idea of worship. However, once we reach such depths we may wonder whether the word secularism has any meaning at all and whether we should not use another word in order to reserve the term secularism for the autonomic reaction, and, thus, not allow it to be used for the ontonomic attitude.

Whatever terminological policy we adopt, I feel that one point has to be made. Not only does every man subsist on truth—everything else is simply lack of life, stagnation—but also every culture, every religion and every interpretation of a concept nourishes the lives of its 'believers' with the truth contained within its particular attitude, doctrine, etc. Extrapolated, even in the minds of their supporters, the ideas may be wrong and the attitude false, but existentially the impetus given by the attitude is always a positive and thus a true force. I would like to restrict myself to just one aspect of this complex and delicate problem and apply it to the concept of worship.

It is along these lines that I would like to develop a few immediately applicable principles regarding the question of secularization *and* worship.

Chapter 3

WORSHIP

Theological Suggestions

1. THE PRINCIPLE OF COMPLEMENTARITY (WORSHIP TOWARDS AND VERSUS LIFE)

I have submitted a definition of worship as an expression of a belief, but how far does this amount to saying that it should be an expression of the life of a people at a particular moment? If worship is a living expression of a living belief it will be an expression of the life of the people who hold the belief, for life is undoubtedly shaped by beliefs, but it still remains to be seen how far it is a corrective to that life or even an attestation on behalf of another, altogether different, life.

The word 'expression' may sound too passive and too immanent. In order to convey the complementary meaning we might equally have said, 'im-pression'. Worship is that which expresses and 'impresses' a particular belief, that which responds and reacts to a particular belief, coming to it either from the inside or from the outside. In point of fact, if it comes from either side, then neither pure immanence nor pure transcendence is possible. This tension and polarity is what we would like to examine and to examine from a particular point of view.

A few points seem to be acceptable without much controversy: (1) Worship, if it is to be really what it claims to be and also to be of any relevance, has to have a direct bearing on the life of the people. It cannot exist

56

only on the transcendental plane. (2) Worship has to have some distinctive features so as to be not only distinguishable but also effective. To convert the whole world into a temple would not do, and to identify the temple with the world at large would not solve the problem either. If everything is worship, then nothing is worship. In other words, there has to be identity, on the one hand, and difference, on the other.

If we profit from the knowledge of the history of religions we may detect what I would like to call the *law of complementarity*. When the identification between life and worship was taken for granted, i.e., when it went without saying that worship was a function of life and that it was itself a form and indeed the highest form of life, the difference between both was stressed in order to maintain that healthy tension, that complementarity which is necessary if human existence is to be dynamic and not stagnate. When the priest and the monk were part and parcel of society, their estrangement was equally underscored. When the houses were poor, the temples were rich, when everything was tinged with the sacred, worship was set apart within the innermost shrines of the temples, on inaccessible mountain recesses, in monastic enclosures, while its distinctiveness was enhanced by the use of learned and in a way artificial language; the sacred was synonymous with the segregated, the set apart, the unutterable, the transcendent, the difficult (few are those who reach salvation in the opinion of practically all the traditional religions of the World), etc.

There were two main categories for this 'setting apart': time and space. When all was sacred, when the whole pattern of life was wrapped in myth and had constant reference to the transcendent, the forms of worship had to affirm themselves by setting apart some places or times specially dedicated to its exercise: either special times, as any history of religions will tell us: morning and evening (*sandhya*, lauds, vespers), holy and less holy days, feasts, and in general the whole calendar: special places, shrines, rivers, mountains, caves, or simply enclosures, even within cities or other dwelling areas. The vow of stability of the Benedictines, for instance, is more than a pure reaction against the abuse of the wandering monks; it represents the consecration to a holy life as guided by the spacial principles of holiness.

When on the other hand, the difference was considered the basic principle: separation of Church and State, God's and Caesar's different realms, civil and religious life, when the secular, in one word, asserted itself over against the sacred, then the identity was consciously stressed: The real love for God is service to man, godliness is cleanliness, work is worship, the city of God has to be planted here on earth, neither Garizim nor Jerusalem, all the rivers are the Ganges and all water is equally holy, the altar is a simple table and the temple a plain house, Indra is Varuna and all the gods are only names of one and the same Power. And so on. There are many examples.

The immanence-transcendence tension is differently stressed according to this principle of complementarity.

This is done even at the innermost heart of worship itself. The example of Roman Catholic spirituality during the past few centuries is clear enough to need no further explanation: when Holy Week became either pure folk-lore or a non-understandable rite, popular piety was fostered by 'Spiritual Exercises' and retreats of the Ignatian type. When the Latin canonical prayers were no longer understood and more or less reserved for the clerics, recitation of the rosary, novenas and other forms of vocal prayer became popular. When the Mass was reduced to an almost private affair between the priest and

58

God, though the priest was supposed still to represent the people, ascetic and devotional life took other channels, etc.

It is a fact that Christian worship today is estranged from the main currents of life. It is also a fact that many efforts are being made to re-integrate the two.

I may be allowed to formulate two direct consequences of this principle of complementarity:

(a) The Integration of Worship with Ordinary Human Life

Under this heading I would include all efforts to 'humanize' worship. People eat. It is the eating that has to be transformed by the sacramental presence and thus the Eucharist has to regain its symbolism of being a meal. People dance and amuse themselves. Christian worship has here again to recover its aspect of celebration and festivity. People are born, come of age, get married, adopt a profession and die. The sacraments have to sanctify and consecrate these most universal and elemental human acts. The sacraments of Initiation, Maturity, Marriage, etc., must not be simply ceremonies and traditional ritualisms, but have a real bearing on and meaning for these important moments of human existence; in a word, they must really shape them. And just as most of these acts are more than mere momentary occasions, the sacramental life cannot be reduced to a mere solemnity once and for all. In other words, worship has to permeate human life once again and render it more meaningful, enhancing the significance of those acts and also giving the necessary strength (grace) for one to live up to the demands of such a human calling. A whole reform is here demanded.

One of the greatest difficulties is the agricultural background of practically all traditional forms of worship, while in our time life, and especially human life, is dominated by what could be called our *technicultural* environment. Since the last century, the world and in particular the Western world has been the receiver of an overwhelming variety of new techniques which have created this highly 'technological' environment of ours. Now, with few exceptions these technological innovations, whether blessings or curses, have rested on an essentially agricultural pattern which is becoming increasingly weaker. It would be one of the most fascinating roles of real worship to transform the present technological age into a *technicultural* one. By this word, as I have elaborated elsewhere, we do not mean a thorough and ruthless technification or an abandonment of ecological reality. On the contrary, we mean, first of all, the discovery that the earth belongs to the human being, and vice-versa, that the human background today is neither agricultural nor technological, but technicultural: included in this word are of course, the earth and nature, for pure nature and untrodden earth are just as much an illusion as a purely mechanised man. Neither rural nor technical motives alone will do today; neither agri-culture nor techno-logy will suffice. The techniculture that is now timidly dawning could be genuinely human and not at all dehumanizing: though it no longer cultivates the fields of an unspoiled earth, it unites with the pulsation of this macro-anthropo-organism which, though called the cosmos does not exclude that which we refer to as God.

(b) The Introduction of Life into Worship

After all, worship is a human act and not an angelic performance. The symbols have to be real. If there is 'bread' and 'wine', it has to be bread and wine; if there is the kiss of love and embrace of peace, then they must be capable of stopping every form of hatred and of really helping us to convey peace and love to one another; if cleansing of sins, there must be a visible change of life; if prayer to God, it cannot be inhibitory of human action and initiative. Worship cannot be disconnected from ordinary human life and the first condition is that worship be not only alive but part and parcel of life itself. How can I believe that worship is the most important act in my daily life if it has no place in it, or, at best, is only allotted an insignificant corner of my weekly routine just to appease my conscience? If human life today shuns solemnities and splendours, if man's temporal consciousness is no longer dominated by the experience of privileged moments of time then modern worship can only be meaningful and relevant if it descends from the platform of the solemn and the privileged and comes down to man's daily existence. One 'yes' uttered in fear and expectation which is the manifestation more of wishful thinking than of a mature resolution cannot bind man for ever, the act must be re-enacted time and again. This is how a certain mentality speaks of such practises as having more than one sacrament and vow: a fact which I am merely stating without comment.

These two corollaries are inter-related. On the one hand, worship has to permeate ordinary human life and, on the other, real human life has to make worship alive and significant. The symbiosis is a vital and important one. It is also difficult. For centuries, in the West at least, these two realms have existed apart and with little contact. Life has gone its own way while worship has followed its own course. No wonder that talk of estrangement has found such a deep echo.

The problem is difficult but it is also unavoidable. We cannot fall prey to a shallow optimism and go the easy way of wanting worship merely to follow life and, in the last resort, the latest ephemeral fashion. We cannot adopt either the strict and anti-human (if not anti-christian) attitude of considering worship a mere corrective and chastiser of life, and it would be equally one-sided, to say the least, to want to conserve the Latin Liturgy because of the beauties of Gregorian chant, or to want to implant jazz in the Liturgy because of its popular appeal and vitality. The criterion has to be of another order altogether.

It is here that at least a word has to be said regarding that widely held view of life and especially liturgy as a play, as a cosmic play with passion and earnestness but without the ultimately tragic, with rules to be followed but only for the 'time-being'. Liturgy is the re-enactment of the total world-play on a human scale. Life enters into the forms of worship, because worship does not claim anything else than to be the very quintessence of human life, expressing not only its individual symbolism but also its cosmic destiny and vocation.

Let us elaborate somewhat further a number of the implications and difficulties inherent in this principle of complementarity with its double dimension of worship towards and versus life.

2. THE COROLLARY OF UNIVERSALITY AND CON-CRETENESS

The principle of complementarity claims to combine in a harmonic blend two characteristics of every human truth: universality and concreteness. Any value which has no claim to universality within its own sphere can hardly be called a value. A private truth, within its sphere can hardly be called a value. A private truth, like a private language, is a contradiction in terms, truth like language being fundamentally a matter of relationships. Likewise a merely abstract truth with no direct reference to a concrete, human situation, which is neither incarnated anywhere nor possesses a bearing on a particular context, could hardly be called a human truth.

It is the phenomenological as well as theological characteristics of any mature religious attitude to aim at a universal validity without watering down its claim to concreteness. This seems to be the philosophical 'translation' of the Incarnation: the revelation of a God in human form, or in other words, the concrete manifestation, incarnation, expression, image of the universal truth, value, God, etc. Although this is, specifically, Christian terminology, one could equally make use of the terms and images of other religious traditions, for this phenomenon seems to be present in almost every one of them.

No attitude can be called really Christian if it ceases to lay claim to one or other of these apparently opposing features. The tension is obvious. One may easily be universal, all-embracing, tolerant and so on, but only if so one generally renounces the concrete, the historical, the corporal and the like. One may equally extol the value of the concrete, the individual, the fact, the historical, but disregard the reality or importance of the mythical, the universally valid, the global. Ultimately the polarity is everywhere preserved, yet Indian religions unmistakably represent the former trend, whereas Semitic religions are typical representatives of the latter. It is a fact also that, with a few exceptions, Christian doctrine has emphasized mainly the semitic trend and for obvious historical reasons, but I would consider essential to the Christian mystery the harmonious combination of both aspects, Christianity being a revelation of the theandric nature of reality.

The tremendous challenge of these corrolaries is that worship cannot be sectarian, cannot exclude all those who live and work together with me, while at the same time it has to be concrete and meaningful to the individual person. And this is the enormous difficulty in a pluralistic society. Worship should be the inspiring force in any work, be the guiding principle of the eight or so hours of our daily activity; but how can it be this if we share this activity with people who do not concede such a worship or find it meaningless or even repulsive? If we insist, it would defeat the purpose. Have we then to worship privately? (must we be content with a short, private prayer before we begin work or take a meal or whatever? Or proceed with a merely private and internal intention? Or have we to find new universally accepted or at least acceptable forms of worship? The Flag, the perpetual flame in front of the Unknown Soldier, the Constitution, the Founder of the Nation or the Liberator, or Man on the Moon; what are the Universal symbols of today?

God was, once upon a time, the universally recognized symbol and in Europe until very recently international declarations and treatises of Peace were signed in the name of the Holy Trinity. To introduce life into forms of worship does not mean simply to make the music more exciting, it means to introduce universal or rather—and the correction is all important—universally recognized or at least acceptable values into forms of worship.

The task may be and indeed is very difficult, but it is *imperative* on the one hand, and *not impossible* on the other.

It is *imperative*, for without a universal liturgy no human fellowship and real fraternity is possible. Probably one of the reasons (effect or cause, I leave it open) of the deep crisis of the United Nations is that it could not or knew not how to develop a really common and thus universal and meaningful liturgy, cult, worship. Over against a really universal horizon all religions are

64

sectarian and all humanisms shallow. Let us squarely face the challenge if we want seriously to tackle the problem of worship in a secular age.

In order to achieve a full human life I have to live in communion with my fellow beings. Man cannot live, nor surely, survive, in isolation. But there is no real human communication unless the roots of human existence are laid bare and communion is established at that profundity. Communion means something more than just exchanging information. In other words, unless the communication is religious there is no real human communion; unless there is *communicatio in sacris* (in the classical theological language) there is no communication, but only an exchange of goods or words or a simple acknowledgement of the presence of the other in order to have freedom to proceed further without obstacles. The usual forms of greeting were all religious and still are, when used in a profound way, even if we no longer recognise the immediate meaning of the words or gestures.

While affirming both that real human communication is communion in our deepest nature, even if we do not share the same opinions or have the same value-judgements, and that this communication is religious communication, I am making a sort of definition or, at least, a phenomenological description of what a religious encounter is—and indeed of what religion is. If religion has any value it is at this level that it is significant. That ultimate layer of human existence where our destiny is at stake, where our ultimate concerns are expressed, where our life is really lived and our ideals are nurtured, that is the realm of religion and if any encounter takes place at this level it is a religious encounter, whatever the religious affiliation or ideas of the people involved may be.

It is obvious that if worship is to be relevant for our times and is not to be relegated to a private affair or to the enjoyment and benefit of a select few, it has to achieve again, not only that universality but those depths at which the human being is really and ultimately what he is meant to be. I am fully aware of the weighty consequences of this view, but unless we get at the root of the matter all our discussion is bound to be mere small talk on procedures.

This task of finding universal symbols is, at the same time, *not impossible*, for in spite of human divergencies and religious discrepancies not only is human nature the same but also the human venture is one and the same. It is here that we may discover the fundamental role of worship in finding or almost creating existential convergences among the people of a certain cultural area. Religion has too often been identified with orthodoxy, precisely because what I would like to call *orthopraxis* was taken for granted. We are more aware today than a century ago that the fundamental dimension of religion is not the realm of ideas (and thus of the right ideas, the correct doctrine, orthodoxy), but of the right and authentic actions leading man to his goal: what traditionally would be called the sacred action, the cult or ritual by which man reaches his destiny. The priority given to orthodoxy was the reason why those who refused to share doctrinal agreement were not admitted to share the same cult, for then it would not actually be the same cult, it would be participating in an error. We are entering a very delicate, but nonetheless urgent problem.

If the emphasis, on the other hand, is put on the orthopraxis, that is, on the intention of performing the right action directly or indirectly conducive to the fulfilment of man, of his goal in life, or however we may like to word it, then we can perform a meaningful act even if we do not share the same doctrinal system and do not agree in our ideas: we do not excommunicate one another and we realise that we are taking part in something which somehow transcends us all.

The reform here, or rather the conversion, will have to be radical. God was for a long time in almost all cultures and religions a universally accepted name, standing for the ultimate, though many different systems or religions offered various explanations of the nature of the God-head. It seems to be a fact that the name of God does not convey this meaning today. It seems on the contrary, to be, a rather controversial name and many would like to divide mankind into 'believers' and 'non-believers', understanding by the former those who maintain that they believe in a personal God, and by the latter, those who affirm that they do not believe in such a divine person. I submit that the moment it is accepted that the idea of a personal God can be meaningless to somebody and that at the same time the core of religion lies in orthodoxy, one is not only condemning all who do not think in this way, but one is making God a superfluous hypothesis negating by this very fact the fundamental divine function of being to be the ultimate and necessary ground of everything. God can no longer be the foundation of thinking if I recognize the possibility of a real thinking which denies this very foundation. A real God, the foundation of everything, including the thinking of those who deny his existence, can obviously not be denied by any thinking and much less be made the starting point of a division among men. This God whom some affirm and some deny cannot be the God of those who acknowledge him under a particular conceptual garb.

The Anselmian *id quo magis cogitari nequit* means here *id sine quo cogitari nequit*, having as immediate consequence that it is *id quod cogitari nequit*[1]. In the scientific words of the History of Religions I would simply say that no idea of God can replace the myth of God and that only the latter can be a universal ground for those who live in that myth. But all this was here only parenthetical.

I would however add this, to avoid misunderstanding: I am not denying the right and perhaps the convenience, for Christians or for followers of any religion, of practising the rites of their religion according to the patterns fixed by authority and tradition. I am only saying, first, that this has little to do with worship in a secular age, because it seems to ignore the fact that our age has ceased to be religiously uniform, even among those who belong to the same confession; and, second, that the challenge that Christian, or any faith for that matter, has primarily to face today is that of universality, i.e. of being able to express in a universal way the concrete values it is embodying. Either we identify the Christian *fact* with historically existing Christianity—and then we have one religion among others, with no more rights than any of them, or we believe that the Christian mystery bears a universal message capable first of all of being understood, and then followed by any man regardless of his colour, culture, and religion. If this is the case, it is the task of Christians with such a conviction to look for forms of expressing this universal belief in manners appropriate to the secular man of today. I do not think I am watering down the Christian message; on the contrary, I am convinced that this is the only way in which it

---

[1] 'That better than which cannot be thought', 'That without which no thinking can be performed'. 'That which cannot be thought'.

can be loyal to its very *kerygma*: the good and astounding news of liberation. It is about this liberation of Christ that I would like to speak in the last section of this introductory essay.

3. THE NEW NIGRICS IN CONTRAST TO THE OLD RUBRICS

First of all I would like to mention a general idea in anthropology regarding the form and content of worship. In the parlance of Western Europe from the XIV century onwards, but which was generalized only in the XVII, the so-called 'rubrics', (because they were written in red), stand for the external acts accompanying the internal acts of the divine service. Set alongside the rubrics is the proper text of worship, which because it was generally written in black, I here call the *nigrics*. The history of the development of worship in any religion shows an almost constant pattern, which I may be permitted to sum up like this: at the beginning rubrics and nigrics were regarded indiscriminately. Their forms and contents were not separable and were barely distinguished, the external act having as much importance as the internal one, if not more. Any sacramental theology could offer us examples and reflections illustrating how the sacramental act is a special blending of internal and external action. In a fascinating process in which the whole of human conciousness is involved, rituals are gradually interiorized until eventually, intention, which is often termed faith, gains the upper hand, to such an extent indeed that it endangers the material, external aspect of the act. A compromise then occurs and there is a certain balance, not always easy to keep, between the nigrics and the rubrics. The history of cult shows that sometimes it has been the rubrics which have in some way created the nigrics, i.e. the external actions have often conditioned the prayers and attitudes of worship. At other times it has been the nigrics, the intention and the conscious effort, which have sought for ways of expression. To say that the nigrics have to create the rubrics would be to approach the question too intellectually and theoretically as if the creative force of man resides in his mind alone, but it is equally one-sided to maintain that the rubrics have the initiative and that the nigrics have only to fill up, as it were, the spaces created by the external and spontaneous manifestations of worship. The contemporary mind moreover, can probably no longer accept a mythopoietic period in which the 'god' himself reveals the ways in which he wants to be worshipped. This, in my opinion is where the real difficulty lies. Worship is neither just a 'receiving' from the 'god' nor simply an activity of our 'human' being. A purely 'god' given form of worship is hardly acceptable today, while a merely humanly concocted form of worship would defeat its own purpose and be of no use to man. The theandric aspect of worship here reappears. By theandric I do not mean the dichotomy of a divine initiative received by a human receptivity, but the non-dualistic experience of an act, which is all-in-one and more than human. These remarks may suffice to indicate the enormous complexity and, at the same time, the urgency of the problem of worship. We are not dealing with a merely pastoral problem of how best to adapt old 'stuff' to the new generation; we are rather struggling with the problem of human self-understanding at its deepest level.

I would like to suggest a few points, placed under three headings as an aid to easier comprehension and discussion.

(a) The New Rubrics
Any religious tradition has developed over the centuries a

number of regulations and canons aiming at crystallizing the spirit and practice of true worship so as to inspire and facilitate it. There exist religious traditions for which the rubrics are essential to the worship. The *mîmâmsaka* interpretation of the Vedic sacrifices or the prevailing post-tridentine Roman Catholic insistence regarding the specific words of the Eucharistic consecration offer two clear instances of what I am trying to say: if certain rubrics are not followed the worship is invalid.

It is easy to criticise obsolete rubrics and to show the danger of superstition or even magic once the rubrics gain the upper hand in worship. But it may be equally short-sighted to pretend to be able to dispense with any ritual injunction. This is not the occasion to enlarge on the anthropological statement that man is a ritual being and that he cannot live without rites. The incontrovertible fact, however, is that the majority of those fundamental rites which were once taken for essential rules of the human game are to-day apparently being contested. Now, a general characteristic of any authentic rite is that it belongs to what I have called elsewhere the 'collective conscious' (treasure or deposit) of a certain human group. Precisely because of this, once a rite has become *self*-conscious and has been brought to the light of critical examination, it cannot survive unchanged and either simply fades away or changes from the living rite that it once was, into a lifeless piece of ritualism to be maintained at all costs by a minority which regard themselves as the elect.

One can easily understand the indignation of the younger generation when they see their elders, for example, engaged in seriously discussing whether or not a little water is needed in the chalice for the Eucharistic consecration, or whether the criteria for Christian inter-communion lie in doctrinal refinements of Scholastic theology, thus overlooking the fact that the crisis of the rubrics is a crisis of universally recognized symbols and not of the peculiar meaning of some specific symbol, important as this may be in a particular context.

Without any further intention than that of giving some examples and offering tentative suggestions, I venture to submit some of the fundamental rubrics for authentic liturgy in our time.

We have already defined worship as a symbolic act expressing a certain belief. The Christian rubric par excellence will be that which symbolizes the saving act of Christ. Now this act can be symbolized in a variety of ways: a man in a cubicle of 2 metres square, murmuring some sacred words in remembrance of the Passion of Christ or the Christian priest, under a regime of strict persecution, passing and breaking some biscuits for his fellow Christians at a political gathering, the only place where they could safely meet, or a crowd shouting for joy that Christ is risen and that they have been visited by him in their innermost hearts . . . I am not passing any judgement, I am not entering into the contents, into the nigrics, but only into the patterns and symbols capable of expressing the Christian mystery: the rubrics.

Spontaneity I would consider one of the most important rubrics for a real worship in a secular age. Christ saved mankind freely, his acts were spontaneous. He did not act in a drama or fulfil an imposed role. His life was a free human life.

Now, a spontaneous rubric may appear to be a contradiction in terms, for a rubric is considered to be a given pattern according to which the proper act has to be performed or to which the symbolic act has to adapt itself. This is however not the case and is the dichotomy I am reacting against. Let us recall again that the problem of worship is not simply a matter of mere speculative thinking.

72

Under the term spontaneity I understand the use of living symbols, i.e. of symbols which are still felt to be natural and do not need to resort to erudite explanations in order to bring their meaning to the mind and heart of man. The use of saliva and shouting out against an evil and a 'dirty spirit' may not convey today what it did centuries ago, to give just one example.

It belongs to the very morphology of symbols to convey spontaneously the message they embody. Eating and drinking, for instance, are symbolic acts and can easily be used to convey the whole charge of a sacramental message. Wheat and wine, on the contrary may not, perhaps, be able to convey such symbolism forcefully outside the mediterranean cultural area and its colonies. Genuflecting or kissing similarly may be spontaneous forms of reverence and love in certain cultures, while they may be meaningless or even repulsive in others.

The rubric of spontaneity would then mean that no symbols are to be imposed and that some may be eventually rejected if they are found to be inconsistent with the rest of the current world-view or not appropriate to the life of the community. This does not mean anarchy. On the contrary, it means a proper orderliness, for anarchy enters automatically the moment that a rule is imposed from outside and is followed only because it is imposed. Neglect or infringements of the rule will immediately follow such an imposition and this will lead to a patchwork tantamount to anarchy. We have many examples of this today.

Spontaneity in rubrics will not only create an atmosphere of freedom and confidence in the 'ecclesia' performing any particular rite, but will also involve something parallel to Christ's injunction to us to abandon a form of worship even if it is already begun and go first to reconcile ourselves with our brethren. Spontaneity will

73

demand authenticity and purity of heart, which is, after all, the most traditional precondition of any form of worship: everywhere we have purification rites before performing the act of worship proper. We need not think of primitive rites only, we may recall the meaning of the confession of sins at the beginning of almost all Christian liturgies.

The rubric of spontaneity does not command: 'be spontaneous' as a sort of injunction to 'keep smiling' while doing what is for the time being written in the smaller rubrics. It does not command 'be spontaneous, only do it willingly.' It is not a piece of pastoral advice to help us adapt ourselves to the prescribed rites. It is rather the injunction to follow the Spirit and allow a living interaction to come into operation, so that the nigrics may build up their corresponding rubrics in a given situation and the rubrics their nigrics.

If the nigrics say, for instance, 'rejoice' or 'lift up your hearts', the rubrics will have to give appropriate expression to the meaning of those nigrics; if the nigrics speak of peace and fraternity it will obviously be strange, to say the least, if the rubrics do not express meaningfully these fundamentally human and religious attitudes, i.e. if differences and injustices within the very congregation are ignored or even still maintained. Once, we may note, the Gospels report a supposedly elaborate and ritualistic Jewish banquet being 'interrupted' by the non-rubrical act of Zacchaeus, the host, giving to the poor half of his riches. I am suggesting that this attitude belongs also to the rubrics of the Liturgy of the New Convenant.

If the rubrics, on the other hand, lead us to express ourselves by gesture, voice or any other type of action, including social and so-called secular actions, if, in fact, we find ourselves involved in any particular activity, spontaneity demands that such actions should be performed with full consciousness of their ever-transcendent, liturgical or sacramental meaning. If I find myself painting, working, dancing eating and so on, the requirement and proof of an integrated life is that all these actions are performed and experienced as more than just 'intranscendental' actions.

How to follow this rubric of spontaneity is not for me now to elaborate. There are already for instance, many trends in more than one church today recognizing the guiding but not the prescriptive character of many norms, leaving optional a series of alternatives according to the circumstances, etc. We may recall the variety of anaphoras in the Orthodox Church, the many patterns of worship in Protestant congregations, the new reform of the liturgy in the Roman Catholic Church, and so on.

Yet the rubric of spontaneity goes far beyond merely allowing for some choice in the performance of a rite. It implies mainly the harmony existent between the symbol and those who use it to symbolize what otherwise would remain unexpressed. Spontaneity, means in terms of Scholastic theology, that no real worship can rely only on the *opus operatum*, disregarding the *opus operantis* and forgetting that the *opus operatum* is not magic, but only a reflection of the *opus operantis Christi*—and Christ has called men only in and for freedom. Spontaneity means, in other words, that authentic worship is fully aware that where there is not free, and thus spontaneous, participation, there is no worship, and that no amount of confidence in the power of the rite itself (*opus operaturm*) can dispense with the free and active involvement (*opus operantis*) of the one who performs the act. No rite is powerful in itself, that is when not connected to man: the Christian effectiveness of a rite depends on the very action of Christ (*opus operantis Christi*).

The rubric of spontaneity will remind us of what was

already traditional in the old Christian liturgies, namely, that all the rubrics and even the nigrics were only suggestions, inspirations, stimulations, starting points, models and patterns to be filled afterwards with flesh and blood, i.e. with life and not with iron rules to be slavishly kept even when one is not convinced of their meaningfulness. The layman has to leave the sacrifice and first get reconciled with his brother, but the priest also has to leave the liturgy and first get reconciled with his 'ecclesia' (however we may interpret it), before he conducts any public worship. Otherwise it would be sheer hypocrisy.

Intimately connected with the first rubric under another aspect, is the rubric of *universality*. Both are linked together. I think that one can venture to affirm that any symbol today which is not universal or capable of being universally accepted can hardly be considered a natural symbol and thus will be of little use for worship.

One of the characteristics of the secular age is its claim to universality. To be sure, one of the appeals of secularism itself is that it is one such symbol. The secular age of secularism does not want to be western or eastern, Christian or Buddhist; it claims to be universal; and it is this claim that gives to secularism so much of its strength.

Any symbol, today, which is meaningful only for a group of men is bound to become sectarian, unfit for worship, especially for Christian worship, which due to its very nature possesses a claim to universality.

The saving action of Christ in which Christians believe and for which they have the support of Scripture and Tradition is truly universal or, to put it in the words of a Council, 'as there never has been, is or shall be a man whose nature was not assumed in Christ, so there never was, shall be or is a man for whom Christ did not die'

(DENZ., 319). A symbol which excludes anybody or makes any type of discrimination can today hardly be called a Christian symbol, or a symbol fit for Christian worship.

The dynamism behind many a change in present-day forms of worship is the new quest of universality. The symbols of the white civilization were at one time taken as universal, but now they have proved not to be so. Latin may once have been a sign of universality, but it has ceased to be so; uniformity was also not so long ago a symbol for universality, but it is being questioned today; centralization was adjudged by the Roman Catholic Church to be the proof and sign of a universal Church, but today it does not have the same ring of truth even in the minds of Roman Catholics; etc.

A universal symbol does not need to be an abstract sign, devoid of life and concreteness. And yet we should not minimize the difficulty in our times of transition of finding or creating universal symbols. When cultures lived in compartmentalized units it was indeed much easier.

Our mentality is still provincial. Yet the whole development of mankind leads us towards a planetarian context. Today it is only against a planetarian horizon that any symbol can be said to be universal. Nobody, to give a very concrete example, contests the right of the first men on the moon to set up their country's national flag, but this action undoubtedly cast a shadow over that fantastic human enterprise which was ready to become a universal symbol. As the news-reports showed the validity of this symbol was spontaneously acknowledged by the greater part of the world. To give another still more delicate example, God was until recently a universal symbol, again for the greatest part of humanity. Today 'God' has almost ceased to be so. And a proof of this is the reluctance the three astronauts felt to speak the name of God when performing an action in the name of the whole human race. In any dialogue between a so-called humanist and a religiously committed person, the former will stress that his ultimate ideal—his God as we could in point of fact say—is greater, broader and thus more valid than the, according to him, narrow conception of a personal God.

The now powerfully emerging ecological conscious-. ness and concern for the earth may provide us with another example. We are in fact witnessing that there are not only symbols that still appeal to man but also that these symbols are universal and genuinely religious. And in this case one can with certainty say that there is no .question of an animistic or so-called 'primitive' return to earth, but a new relationship with the whole of creation. The 'earth' here is not a merely 'natural' or agricultural value but a specific *technicultural* one.

The symbolism of the ontonomic consciousness should not be confounded with the more unconscious symbolism of the heteronomic period. In the ontonomy it is consciousness that discovers its very symbolic charac- ter, for it discovers beings and even pure Being as symbols. This symbolic consciousness differs from the pre-critical awareness and also from the merely critical approach to reality. But I will not pursue these examples further lest we lose the balance of this development.

Let me only give some suggestions as to what I do recognize as universal symbols in contradistinction from particular ones.

Eating, drinking, dancing, celebrating, painting, sing- ing, justice, love, hope, faith, desire, friendship, and the like are undoubtedly universal values, even if one can interpret them in restricted ways.

God, Church, Empire (of many kinds) were, within

certain natural limits, universal values also. They have been superseded by values like Democracy, Independence, Alphabetization, Education, and for some people, Technology, Science, Standard of Living, etc.

A third rubric that should complement these two others is that of *concreteness*. A symbol is only a symbol if it is a concrete symbol and not an abstract word or image. Concreteness here should not be viewed as a negation of the universal but as its (concrete) expression. The symbols of worship cannot be generalizations. They would have no appeal and driving force for the great majority and would also defeat their purpose, which is to lead us beyond, behind, above, higher, further or whatever adverbial metaphor we may care to use.

It would thus be a poor favour to any worshipping community to artificially substitute symbols which we consider obsolete with others that we may personally find more fitting. That community would immediately, as is proved by both past and present experience, invest the new symbols with the old meanings. Real symbols cannot be invented nor manipulated. Their original force is almost incredible. Take for example modern medicines which in countries of the Third World possess the power and efficacity of old idols. Only a short time ago I heard how a neighbour of mine simply swallowed the scrap of paper upon which his medical prescription was written as if it had been the medicine itself. Is it not the transfer of the cult of the Emperor to the cult of national scientific development which explains the amazing phenomenon of post-war Japan? Spanish missionaries arriving in the Philippines did not destroy what, according to them, were the superstitions of the islanders; in practice they substituted the cult of idols by the veneration of Christian saints, kept the old feasts and costumes and tried to give them a Christian motivation. In other countries missionaries followed the so called method of *tabula-rasa*. The results no matter how we judge them, are obvious: in the one case the Christian message was grafted on, while in the other it remained a foreign body.

Emphasis should be laid upon the need for a harmonious combination of universality and concreteness. If the former without the latter is barren and powerless, the latter without the former is sectarian and unjust. Wisdom demands that we discover the concrete in the universal and that we universalize the concrete without getting lost in vague generalizations. The Incarnation, taken as the manifestation of the Absolute in the Relative, offers perhaps the most striking symbol.

This and other considerations lead me to sum up these three rubrics under a single heading and, indeed, they are simply three strands of the same rope. We could express this by saying that it is the rubric of *truthfulness*.

Truthfulness implies a worship in spirit and in truth and represents a correspondence between the rubrics and the nigrics, the meaningfulness of every act because it really symbolizes what we believe. Truthfulness is always spontaneous and almost unconscious. We are convinced of the truth of something, not by means of an elaborate and painful process of syllogistic deduction, but because a simple internal act leads us to be convinced of its truth. Though the way may have been long and even painful, once we arrive at the goal, we get so clear an insight into its truth as to forget the intermediary steps. Because we are convinced of the truth of something we combine, in a manner which the outsider cannot, universality with concreteness. Because we are convinced of the *truth* of something we take it to be universally valid. Because it is *our* conviction it is limited to the horizon of our experience and is thus truly concrete. But because it is our *conviction* and we give our assent only to truth, it is for us the embodiment of truth, partaking in this way both of universality and concreteness.

Under this main rubric of truthfulness I would finally include the temporal dimension of truth. In other words, real worship has to be true to the past as well as the future, while, of course, not forgetting the present. An utterly idolatrous attitude towards the past would not be truthful while equally false would be an attitude which negates the temporal constitution of man and thus under a guise of spontaneity wants to shroud everything with the cloak of the present, ignoring all the other human dimensions.

Another related and important rubric to be noted here, is the rubric of *continuity*, which could equally be called the rubric of *tradition* or *evolution*. This is not the same as constancy or traditionalism, nor is it revolution and rupture. Any kind of worship today cannot simply ignore past centuries with their forms of worship and pretend to start from scratch. This would be, incidentally, the worst form of traditionalism.

In very practical terms this rubric says that any form of Christian worship must, whether in countries with an ancient Christian tradition or in the many Christian enclaves throughout the world, be connected with existing forms of worship while at the same time allowing for evolution, development and change. The reason for this is not only pastoral, that is trying to avoid unnecessarily bewildering the older generation but theological. Christian worship is remembrance as well as expectation, and Christian loyality is extended not only towards the future but towards the past. The speed with which changes need to be made is also an important question, but we are not now discussing Church policies. We are trying only to study the foundations of an authentic worship for our time.

If Christian worship is to avoid being an isolated and sectarian form of worship, it has also somehow to establish the kind of continuity of which we have spoken with all the surrounding forms of worship, including those not belonging to the Christian tradition; history furnishes us with ample proof of this necessity. This rubric is very important today when, on the one hand there is a certain rigidity (now breaking down) inherited from the past two or three centuries and, on the other, the challenge presented by the so-called secular world to all exclusive or particularistic forms of worship. It would be inconsistent to pray *for* others and not to pray *with* them. There would be remnants of a colonialistic and paternalistic attitude to pray *for* the 'heathen' and not to allow them to pray *with* us or even to pray *with them and with their prayers* once we agree that those prayers are acceptable. We may offer an example: the world-wide controversy regarding the 'convenience' or 'congruence' of introducing Sacred Scriptures other than those of the Old and New Testaments into the Christian liturgy. As usual, life and liturgy precede both the law and pure speculative theology.

Paradoxically, no doubt, I should like to emphasize the value of the rubrics and to stress their ontonomic character by introducing a further category, namely, *orthopraxis.*

A healthy reaction against rubricism may very easily become the total anarchy of not accepting any rubric. I would maintain the peculiar ontonomy of the rubrics which signifies a proper balance, with the rubrics not 'bossing' the nigrics about nor the nigrics tyrannizing over the rubrics, as if the function of the rubrics were only to follow blindly what the content of the worship indicated.

I may explain by means of an example the meaning of orthopraxis as a rubric. The nigrics may say, for instance, 'the Lord be with you', or 'let us rejoice' or 'let us have peace with one another'. It is for the rubric to give a concrete and existential expression to the nigrics. Now, it may very well be that the doctrinal implications of the nigrics is that Christ is the Lord, that Joy is the direct fruit of the Easter event and that the Church is the source of real and everlasting peace. Obviously, a full participation in the nigrics is not possible for those who do not believe in their specific assumptions. But when the rubrics translate or express what the nigrics say into living symbols of, say, self-confidence, dance or a particular service to our neighbour, they are not making the assumptions of the nigrics, so that people could in practice share in the Christian worship by participating in the expressions of their Christian neighbours: feeling reassured, dancing, singing, praising or working with them in the many strains and stresses of daily life. This participation in the rubrics without a total acceptance of the nigrics is, in fact, not so odd as it may sound. In any real popular and living religious worship (and this is at the same time a criterion for its authenticity) the rubrics have such a splendour and power of their own that the participants are never simply the exclusive group of the orthodox. For instance, in any pilgrimage or popular feast no matter where Christians, Hindus and Muslims, join together and in fact nobody can stop them. The same is true of any Christian feast in the Middle East or Buddhist celebration in the Far East, and it was not by mere chance that during the Roman Catholic Eucharistic Congress in Bombay a few years ago hundreds of thousands of Hindus received daily Communion. The ritual has a value of its own and this is a fact that cannot simply be overlooked. Let us not forget that worship is not so much an affair of the theologian *qua* theologian, but of the believer and of the full man *qua* man and that we cannot stop life, or limit, artificially or intellectually, the deeper urges of man[1].

Recognition of this fact may give us some guidelines of how, when regulating rubrical advice, to avoid disorder and anarchy and at the same time not impinge on the liberty of the worshipper.

Modern forms of worship should also provide for the participation of those who do not share the orthodoxy of the believers and yet accept the wider rules of the game, as formulated in the rubrics. A delicate, but unavoidable problem.

(b) The New Nigrics

I would like to begin with three rather significant quotations. The first is from Tertullian: "Temples and tombs, we detest equally, we know no kind of altar . . . we offer no sacrifice"[2]. The second is taken from the Arabic Life of Abbot Pachomius: When

---

[1] A few years ago two Roman and theologically very conservative prelates were travelling in a 'mission-country' with a very 'Catholic' couple. Good and sincere Christians as they were, they invited their 'non-Christian' driver, first, to sleep in the hotels and not in the car, then to eat with them and not outside and finally to share comments and friendship with them and not to remain an outcaste. After a few days the driver was also attending Mass-how could they refuse?—and a few days later he was receiving the Eucharist . . .

[2] *De spectaculis,* 13.

approaching the bishop of Diospolis to build up a 'church' in Phboou near their monastery, the monks referred to the Church as 'a festive Hall'.[1] Lastly, some words spoken by the Buddha to a Hindu brahmin ready to perform a certain ritual:

> "I pile no wood for fire or altars;
> I kindle a flame within me.
> Ever my fire burns, ever intense and ardent;
> I, Arahant, work out the life that is holy."[2]

No temples, no tombs, no altars; only a celebration hall, only a burning heart.

I cannot now enter into a discussion as to whether primitive Christianity was so totally iconoclastic, atheistic, and anti-ritualistic as to dispense with a Temple and thus with God (because he who has seen Christ has seen the Father whom nobody can see), with Tombs and thus with the idea of a private after-life, (because eternal life is to know Christ and the Kingdom of God within us), with an Altar and thus with sacrifices (because Christ's sacrifice was unique and in consequence adequate and unrepeatable) and whether all these things surreptitiously crept in again in order to cater to mankind's thirst for the tangible and visible. I am only suggesting that Christian faith, which has throughout the ages developed so many

---

[1] *Vie arabe de Pachome* transl. by E. AMELINARS, p. 567 (apud A. VEILLEUX, *La liturgie dans le cenobitisme pachomien*, Rome (pro-manuscripto), 1967, fol. 200, (a doctoral thesis for the Institute of Liturgy of Coll. Pont. St.Anselmo, Roma).
[2] *Samyutta Nikaya*, I, 169.

forms of worship, is not committed to any of them, and just as the Christian faith has expressed itself in every age through the religious forms of its surroundings, it is capable of finding expression in secular forms or in other appropriate sacred rites (as seems to be the need of the 'Third World'). And this does not proceed from a desire to imitate or to be accommodating, but is due to an internal dynamism towards incarnation. Only the transcendent can incarnate itself in any given situation. I should add at once that we find a parallel dynamism in other religions as well. Though we are here concerned mainly with the Christian aspects of the problem, we should not lose sight of the more general issue.

However this may be, I maintain that today we need a theological anthropology capable of giving shape and meaning to the present content and form of worship.

Because of its anthropological value I would like to sum up now the fundamental acts of worship according to a traditional and ancient pattern.

Devotion (*bhakti*) in all its forms is a fundamental dimension of worship. Man is a feeling and sentient being; he needs to express his urges and his desire to overcome his limitations and shortcomings in one form or other. Life without love is not human life. All forms of love, praise, thankfulness, adoration and celebration belong to this category. I must here refrain, however, from analysing the most suitable forms for our secular society.

I would like only to underline the tremendous importance of the arts and especially of music. It is impossible to achieve an integrated involvement of our whole being if we leave aside not only the sentimental part of ourselves, but the artistic element as well. That the arts in almost all cultures were of sacred origin and connected with worship is a widely acknowledged fact.

The process is obviously now not one of bringing back the arts into the sanctuary, but of drawing forth a total form of human worship as an expression of the integration of man into the whole of reality.

Knowledge (*jnana*) is the second fundamental act of worship. Man is an intellectual being. He wants to know, to study, to grapple with things and problems, to discuss, to have 'dialogue' to decipher the mystery of reality. The possibilities today of integrating the act of knowing into the act of worship are enormous. What, in some Christian circles, is termed Bible-study could be enlarged and deepened. Any word can or could be a revelation of a sort. Under this heading not only study but contemplation is included. This, therefore, implies silence, quiet and an ontological awareness of all that is.

I would like to underline here the importance that knowledge has for worship. Only too often the impression has been given that worship has almost nothing to do with the claims of the intellect and we thus relegate not only science but even theology to, at the most, auxiliary disciplines. If the dance of the body belongs to the integral act of human worship, the intuition of the intellect is no less an essential part of the human being and must also be assumed by worship.

Action (*karma*) is also a fundamental act of worship. Worship is not only related to internal acts or to actions directed towards a sacred and independent transcendence; it is also connected with the actual activity of man on earth. It is under this heading that the main category of the sacrifice should also be understood. The building of the city of man coalesces with the building of the city of God, when it is realised that the movement of the incarnation, which connects the transcendent with the immanent, is, in fact, continued by any action which re-enacts this fundamental act of human and cosmic existence.

Again, emphasis should equally be put on the activity of man as *consecratio mundi*, to use a formula which was much in vogue some years ago. Perhaps one of the most important activities of man today and of Christians in a very special way consists in a total and personal engagement in favour of those people, groups, nations or races which need in one way or another a helping hand in order to live a more just and human life. Worship is not merely an aristocratic act or an intellectual or artistic luxury, which could at best be justified as providing force and inspiration for other types of work which man feels he cannot leave undone. Worship includes action as well as the two other elements just mentioned.

Following another traditional pattern I could equally have said that worship has to embrace the beautiful, the true and the good. Without a harmonious integration of these three elements human worship will always fall short of its nature and role.

If the above-mentioned anthropological pattern is not completely wrong, then it is necessary to look for an adequate theology of worship stressing these three points in a balanced way. Christian worship should then provide an opportunity for expressing all the feelings of gratitude, repentance, love and admiration that we shelter in our hearts. Celebration, in one word, is an essential part of worship. Moreover the stress could easily be laid upon the positive feelings of the human heart and Christian spirituality could then cease to be jealous of the achievements of man, which it sometimes is, and stop considering him albeit almost unconsciously, as a rival to God. The *magnalia Dei* are always performed *per homines*, and we should not make much of an issue of whether these men are part of our confessional group or not. It is not merely a question of being witty and saying: 'thy Will be done "on the moon and on earth as in heaven" ' but of worshipping together and of recognising that in every human act there is always something bigger and deeper involved, for good or for bad. Any act of worship should be a deepening of our feelings, an awareness of the tremendous weight of everything. From this point of view, worship could be described as those acts by which we express our stepping out of the banal.

Along with this the intellectual and scientific aspect of worship could be developed. Worship is not only to sing, to pray for mercy or to feel emotionally aroused. It is also, and for many people mainly, to study, to contemplate, to be quiet, in public or in private. Could not the strenuous and magnificent scientific effort of the world today be assimilated and integrated into an act of worship?

To worship, finally, implies 'to do', to work and to collaborate in the construction of the city of man, being at the same time very conscious that this city has a dimension which transcends what is visible at first sight, that the city of God is not a second city, but the real world of which the appearance is precisely this, our visible world. To build up, to discover, to create, to accelerate the human process or the coming of the Kingdom—or whatever expression we may here choose —this too is the function of worship today. The whole of Christian sacramental theology could find here an immense field of exploration and the classical conception of sacrifice in practically all religions is, in fact, intimately connected with this aspect of worship. The ultimate function of sacrifice is to let the whole world reach its destination, to recreate the world, to let time, the *saeculum*, continue, thanks to the efforts of man, who is an active carrier and forgert not simply the passive sufferer of karmic existence.

(c) Worship in a Secular Age

Here, a word has to be said on worship, which no amount of talk about secularization should overshadow. There is a radical dimension in any authentic and profound worship, which touches the roots of the secular, i.e., of the world at its core. Traditional parlance has often called this the ontological or the vicarious aspect of worship. We could equally have termed it the cosmic-personal aspect or the theandric dimension which, to our mind, is a more apt phrase. No act of true worship can be individualistically performed. Worship, as we already said, is ultimately neither collective nor individualistic: it is personal. We understand by person that real crossing of karmatic lines, or real processes which give birth to a spark of consciousness.

Concentrating exclusively on this point, we could describe this aspect of worship by saying that it is the act by which the person cultivates his center and consequently that act by which the person participates in the core of all reality, shares on that deepest level with his fellow-beings and is in communion with the entire universe. Worship is that act by which the person overcomes not only solipsism and isolation, but also the infertile activism of pure agitation and the barren superficiality of an inauthentic existence. In an age in which the inflation of information has almost suceeded in paralysing normal reactions and in which it is factually impossible to 'know' all that is going on, or to master all that has been said on a particular subject, or, indeed, fully comprehend any human field, or respond to all internal and external calls, that aspect of worship which puts us in communication with the centre of the human cosmic or

90

even divine existence becomes more and more vitally and psychologically necessary. Ontology here redeems psychology. I am not saying that worship is a substitute or a consolation for the fact that I am not at the centre of the decision-making agencies of this world, and certainly worship makes no claim to be able to influence them by means of some novel brand of white magic. But I am, on the other hand, emphasizing that an act of worship places man both at the centre of his own and of cosmic existence, however he may like to interpret it. I am stressing the fact that real worship does not dream of 'influencing', because it knows itself to be at a level in which 'influence' has little meaning. Real worship can only begin where one has resisted the temptation of trying to gain the whole world by 'worshipping' an idol. The idol need not always take the form of Satan, nor 'the world' always be called Jerusalem. The 'power' of worship is that it renders powerless the 'powerful' because it has discovered that his 'power' is no real power in so far as it is deemed to be 'his'. Our concern here, however, is not with worship as such but only with the humble 'and' linking our two main concepts.

How am I, a man living in the middle of my age—*saeculum*— to express my faith today? This may be a concrete way of approaching the problem.

Summing up what I have said and also all that I would still like to say, I shall comment upon just one idea. Christian worship should be led and inspired by the living symbol of Jesus, but Jesus was not Christocentric, nor did he allow himself to be worshipped.

The principle of complementarity to which we have alluded should find here its best application. While bearing in mind people and ages that have stressed almost exclusively, the other-worldly aspect of worship, Christian worship must stress service to this world.

Bearing also in mind those for whom the transcendent aspect has been diluted into a mere projection of personal impotence, Christian worship should give expression to man's inner and constitutive urge towards something which remains for ever beyond him. For those who are world-ridden and enmeshed in the net of immediate and purely temporal realities, worship should stress the *sursum corda* of real transcendence, which is not escapism, but a realisation of the true and ultimate human condition. For those who claim to be secularists, humanists, atheists, an authentic worship should be equally meaningful because in contrast to doctrinal attitudes it would not quarrel about conceptions, world views and ideologies, but would simply express the innermost urges of the human being and not only find an outlet for them but a real and creative manifestation of them: not everybody can worship God as Creator, but hardly anybody will not join in a manifestation expressing the Glory and Splendour of the whole or of a part of this creation (whatever name we may give to it).

The theandric unity of Christ requires this balance, which is far from being a grey mediocrity or a middle way between two human risks. On the contrary, the extremes are nothing but lop-sided versions of the fullness of the theandric reality of every man revealed in Christ.

In the light of this how do I envisage Christian worship in our times? I am not discussing whether our epoch is a secularized epoch or not. For me secularization represents the regaining of the sacramental structure of reality, the new awareness that real full human life is worship, because it is the very expression of the mystery of existence. Man is priest of the world, of the cosmic sacrament and we are closer today to accepting this truth also, that he is the prophet of this universe of ours, the celebrant of the sacrament of life and the ambassador of the realm of the Spirit. Worship in this context should not appear an escapism inhibiting our ideals and ambitions, nor an excuse for non-action or not doing what is at hand to be done, but as the integration of all dimensions of life, as the constant 'plus' of matter, when we are being too spiritual, when our sentiments dominate us, of spirit, when the intellect or the body take the upper hand. Worship is neither an interested act asking of a *deus ex machina* what we cannot get by ourselves, nor a superfluous action of a spiritual aristocracy ready to sing or to thank or to ponder, whereas the majority are working, suffering or simply striving. On the contrary, worship, unlike theology, which is the conscious passage from mythos to logos, from unreflecting beliefs to self-critical and intellectually formulable ultimate convictions, represents the espousal of *myth* and *logos*: a marriage which can only take place in the *spirit*. Worship is not the denial of our human condition but the acceptance of it, without allowing ourselves either to be cowed or alienated by pride. Our human condition is in and through worship realistically accepted, neither ignored nor despised. Worship represents neither evasion, nor complacency, but that human, and, I would say, that theandric act—for which faith, hope and love are essentially required—and which, while accepting our human condition, sets us on the path to redeeming it by a transfiguration which Christians well know is visible only in 'Taboric' moments, but which illumines and carries this tremendous experience of being a theandric being.

And as for the *how*, that is one of the reasons why these ideas are assembled here merely to be scattered to the four winds . . .

BIBLIOGRAPHY

The recent literature on Liturgical renewal alone would embrace over a thousand entries. Mention of well-known and specialised Periodicals is omitted. The present selection is governed by three criteria: to make available the titles of:

(a) some of the most representative works on the specific topic of Secularization and Worship.

(b) others relating to areas which though closely connected are generally less well known to the 'Liturgist'.

(c) those studies known to me and directly or indirectly utilised in my essay on Secularization and Worship.

ALLMEN, J.J. *Worship: Its Theology and Practice.* Oxford (University Press), 1965.

ANTHOLOGIE *Les dances sacrées,* Paris (Seuil) 1963.

ARTZ, M. *Justice and Mercy: Commentary on the Liturgy of the New Year and the Day of Atonement.* New York (Holt, Rinehart and Winston), 1963.

AUBREY, E.E. *Secularism. A Myth.* New York (Harper and Brothers), 1954.

AUDET, J.P. "Le sacré et le profane. Leur situation en christianisme". *Nouvelle Revue Theologique,* 79, Paris (1957), 33-61.

BACKMAN, E.L. "Religious dances in the Christian Church and in Popular Medicine" (transl. by E. CLAS-

Bibliography

SEN, from the Swedish), London (Allen and Unwin), 1952.

BASCOM, W.R. "The Myth. Ritual Theory", *Journal of American Folklore*, Boston LXX (1957), 103-114.

BELLAH, R.N. "Religious Evolution", *American Sociological Review*, XXIX Chicago, (1964), 358-374.

——, (Editor) *Religion and Progress in Modern Asia.* New York (The Free Press), 1965.

BELSHAW, C.S. "The Significance of Modern Cults in Melanesian Development" *Australian Outlook*, IV Sidney, (1950) 116-125.

BERGER, P. *The Sacred Canopy. Elements of a Sociological Theory of Religion.* Garden City, New York, (Doubleday), 1967, and London (Faber) as *The Social Construction of Reality.*

——, *A Rumor of Angels. Modern Society and the Rediscovery of the Supernatural.* Garden City, N. York (Doubleday), and London (Allen Lane) 1970.

BERKHOFFER, Jr., R.F. *A Behavioral Approach to Historical Analysis* New York (Free Press), 1969.

BIRNBAUM, W. 'Das Kultusproblem und die Liturgischen Bewegungen des 20. Jahrhunderts", *Die deutsche katholische liturgische Bewegung.* Tübingen (Katzmann).

BLACKFRIARS *Mystery and Mysticism. A Symposium.* "Blackfriars", London, 1956. Chapters by: BOUYER, CERFAUX, HISLOP, LEONARD, PLE, etc.

BLEEKER, C.J. (Editor) *Anthropologie religieuse. L'homme et sa destinée à la lumière de l'histoire des religions*, articles by: PETTAZZONI, PIDOUX, FILLIOZAT, FRAUWALLNER, SCHIMMEL, Leiden (Brill) 1955.

BOGLER, Th. "Das Sakrale im Widerspruch", *Leacher Hefte, 41*, Maria Laach (1967).

——, *Spiel und Feier*, Maria Laach, 1955.

BOUYER, L. *La Bible et l'Évangile—Le sens de l'Ecriture du Dieu qui parle au Dieu fait homme.* Paris (Cerf) 2nd. edition. 1953.

—— *Le Mystère pascal.—Paschale Sacramentum.* Paris (Cerf) 3rd. edition, 1950.

—— *Le Rite et l'homme. Sacralité naturellé et liturgique.* Paris (Cerf), 1962.

——, *Liturgical Piety.* Notre Dame, Ind. (University of Notre Dame) 1966.

BREASE, G. "The City in Newly Developing Centuries", *Reading on Urbanism and Urbanization.* Engle- ·wood, Cliffs, N.J. (Prentice Hall), 1969.

BREEN, Q. *Christianity and Humanism* (Wm. B. Eerdmans), 1968, Grand Rapids.

BRENNER, S.F. *Ways of Worship for New Forms of Missions.* New York, (Friendship Press), 1968.

BROWN, N.O. *Love's Body.* New York (Random House), 1966.

BUYTENDIJK, F.J. *Wesen und Sinn des Spieles.* Berlin, 1933

CAILLOIS, R. *L'Homme et le sacré.* Paris (Gallimard) 3rd. ed. 1950.

Man and the Sacred (Translation). Illinois, (Free Press) 1950.

CAMPBELL, J. "The Secularization of the Sacred" in *The Religious Situation 1968* edited by D.R. CUTLER, Boston (Beacon) 1968, pp. 601-638.

CASEL, O. *Mysterium des Kommenden.* Paderborn (Bonifacius), 1952.

——, *Das christliche Opfermysterium. Zur Morphologie und Theologie des eucharistischen Hochgebetes.* Graz . . . (Styria) 1968.

——, *Das christliche Kultmysterium.* Regensburg (Pustet) 4 ed. 1960.

CAZENEUVE, J. *Les dieux dansant à Cibola: Le Shalako des Indiens Zunis.* Paris (Gallimard) 1957.

CHILDRESS, J.F. & HARNED D.B. *Secularization and the Protestant Prospect.* (The Westminster Press), Philadelphia, 1970.

COX, H. *The Secular City.* New York (Macmillan) 1965.

——, *A feast of fools.* Cambridge, Mass (HUP) 1969.

CULLMANN, O. *Early Christian Worship.* London (SCM) 1966 (VI printing).

CUTLER, D.R. (editor of) *The Religious Situation: 1968*, Boston, (Beacon), 1968.

DANIELOU, J. *Primitive Christian Symbols* (Translation). London (Burns & Oates).

——, *Sacramentum Futuri. Etudes sur les origines de la typologie biblique. (Etudes de Théologie Historique)*, Paris (Beauchesne) 1950.

——, *Sacramento y Culto según los Santos Padres* (Translation). Madrid (Guadarrama), 1962.

DAUMAL, R. *Bharata. L'origine du Théatre. La Poésie et la Musique en Inde.* (Traduction de textes sacrés et profanes). Paris (Gallimard) 1970.

DAVIES, J.G. *Worship and Mission.* London (S.C.M.) and New York (Associate Press). 1966

——, *Dialogue with the World.* London (SCM), 1967.

——, *Secular Use of Church Buildings.* London (SCM) and New York (Holt, Rinehart and Winston) 1968.

DEBUYST, F. "Feast Days and Festive Celebrations: Forstaster of Full Communion", *Concilium.* Nijmegen, IX/4 (Nov. 1968), 5-9.

DODDS, E.R. *The Greeks and the Irrational.* Berkeley (University California Press), 1966.

EBELING, G. "Das Verständnis von Heil in säkularisie-
ster Zeit", *Kontexte*, 4 (1967, 5-14).

EGGAN, F. "Social Anthropology and the Method of
Controlled Comparison", *American Anthropologist,* LVI
Washington, (1954) 743-763.

ELIADE, M. "Images et Symbols, Essais sur le symbolism magico-religieux" *Les Essais LX*, NRF Paris
(Gallimard) 1952.

———, *Mythes, Rěves et Mystères.* Paris (Gallimard),
1957.

———, *Aspects du Mythe.* Paris (Gallimard), 1963.

———, *Myth and Reality* (Translation). New York,
(Harper and Row), 1964.

ENCYCLOPEDIA BRIT. "Should Christianity be Secularized. A Symposium" *The Great Ideas Today*, 1967.

EVANS-PRITCHARD, E.E. *The Institutions of Primitive
Society.* Oxford (Basil Blackwell), 1956.

———, *Theories of Primitive Religion.* (Oxford University
Press), 1965.

FENN, R.K. "*The Secularization of Values. An Ana-
lytical Framework for the Study of Secularization.*"
JSSR VIII/1 (Spring, 1969) pp. 112-124.

FERGUSSON, H. *Modern Man: His Belief and Behav-
ior.* New York (A.A. Knopf & Co., Inc.,) 1936.

FINGARETTE, H. "Human Community as Holy Rite:
an interpretation of Confucius Analects", Cambridge,
Mass. *Harvard Theological Review*, 59 (1966) 53-67.

FORSTER, K. & SCHMAUS, M. (Editors) *Des Kult
und der heutige Mensch.* Munchen (Hueber), 1961.

FORSTNER, D. *Die Welt des Symboles.* 2nd.
ed.—1967.

GEERTZ, C. "Ritual and Social Change: A Javanese

Example", *American Anthropologist*, Washington, LIX (1957), 32-54.

GEFFRE, C.J. "Entsakralisierung und Heilung" *Concilium* Nijmegen, 2 (1966), 708-718.

GOGARTEN, F. *Verhängnis und Hoffnung der Neuzeit, Die Säkularisierung als theologisches* Problem, Stuttgart, 1953.

GOODY, J. "Religion and Ritual: The Definitional Problem". *British Journal of Sociology*, XII (1961), 142-164.

GRAND-MAISON, J. *Le Monde et le sacré. I—Le sacré*, Paris, 1966.

GUARDINI, R. *Glaubenserkenntnis.* Basel (Hess), 1945

——, *I santi segni* (Translation) Brescia (Morcelliana), 4 ed., 1954.

——, *Freiheit-Gnade-Schicksal*, München, 1948 (Kösel-Verlag)

——, *Voschule des Betens* (Benziger) 3rd. ed. 1952.

——, *Unterscheidung des Christlichen* (Gesammelte Studien: 1923-1963) Mainz (M. Grünewald), 1963.

——, *Interpretation der Welt.* Festschrift zum 80 Geburtstag, edited by H. Kuhn, H. Kahlefeld and K. Foster, etc. Würzburg (Echter) 1965.

GUSDORF, G. *L'expérience humaine du Sacrifice.* Paris, (Presses Universitaires de France) 1948.

HARRISON, J.E. *Ancient Art and Ritual.* New York (H. Holt), 1913.

HENNINGER, "Uber Frühlingsfeste bei den Semiten" in *Verbo Tuo* Festschrift St. Augustin, Siegburg, 1963.

——, "Das Menschenopfer für den Arabern" *Anthropos*, 53 (1958), 721-805.

HERSKOVITS, M.J. "African Gods and Catholic Saints in New World Religious Belief", *American Anthropologist*, XXXIX Washington, (1937), 635-643.

HOMANS, G.C. "Anxiety and Ritual: The Theories of Malinowski and Radcliffe-Brown", *American Anthropologist,* Washington, (1941), 164-172.

HOOKE, S.H. *Myth and Ritual,* London (Oxford U. Press) 1933

HORTON, R. "A definition of Religion and its Uses" *Journal of the Royal Anthropological Institute,* XC (1960), 201-226.

HOSELITZ, B.F. & MOORE, W.E. (Editors) "Industrialization and Society" *Proceedings of the Chicago Conference on Social Implications of Industrialization and Technical Change,* (1960), Unesco (Mouton), 1963 (2nd. ed. 1966).

HUBER, C. "Speaking about God in a Secular World" *IDO-C.* Rome (Editorial Note) Nr. 68, 15/16—(IV/1968).

HUIZINGA, J. *Homo ludens.* Boston (Beacon) 1955.

JAMES, E.O. *Seasonal Feasts and Festivals.* New York, (Barnes & Noble), 1961.

JUNG, C.G. *Symbols of Transformation.* Princeton, (Princeton Univ. Press), 1967.

KORVIN-KRASINSKI, C. *Mikrokosmos und Makrokosmos in religionsgeschichtlicher Sicht.* Dusseldorf, Paulus-Verlag— 1960.

LANGER, S.K. *Philosophy in a New Key—A Study in the Symbolism of Reason, Rite and Art.* Cambridge (Harvard University Press) 1942 (Mentor Book 1948).

LEACH, E.R. "Two Essays on the Symbolic Representation of Time" *Rethinking Anthropology.* London (Athlone Press, University of London), 1961

LEEUW, G. van der *Sakramentales Denken. Erschein-*

*ungsformen und Wesen des ausserchristlichen und christ-
lichen Sakramenten.* Kassel (Stander), 1959.

————, *Sacred and Profane Beauty* (trans. David Green).
New York (Holt, Rinehart and Winston) 1963.

LEEUWEN, A.T. *Prophecy in a Technocratic Era.* New
York, (Charles Scribner's Sons), 1968.

LEIST, F. *Kultus als Heilsweg,* 1949.

LENGELING, E.J. "Sakral-Profan. Berich über die
gegenwästige Diskussion", *Liturgischer Jahrbuch,*
Münster, 18/3 (1968) 164-188.

LEVI-STRAUSS, C. "The Structural Study of Myth",
Structural Anthropology. New York (Basic Books)
1963.

————, *La doctrine du sacrifice dans les Brāhmaṇas.* Paris
(PUF), 2nd. ed. 1966.

LEWIS, O. "Comparisons in Cultural Anthropology"
Yearbook of Anthropology, 1955, ed. W.L. THOMAS,
Jr., New York (Wenner Gren Foundation for Anthropo-
logical Research), 1955.

LOEN, A.E. *Säkularisation, Von der wahren Vorsuss-
etzung und angeblichen Gottlosigkeit der Wissenschaft.*
München (Kaiser) 1965.

————, *Secularization, Science without God?* Philadelphia, Penn. (Westminster Press), 1967.

LUBBE, H. *Säkularisierung. Geschichte eines ideenpoli-
tischen Begriffs,* Freiburg (Alber), 1965.

LUCKMANN, Th. *The Invisible Religion.* New
York (Macmillan). 1967.

LYONNET, St. "La nature du culte dans le N.T."
Vatican II. La liturgie après Vatican II, Paris, (1967),
357-384.

MACQUARRIE, J. *God and Secularity.* London (Lutter-
worth), 1968.

MAERTENS, Th. *Heidnisch jüdische Wurzeln der*

christlichen Feste, Mains (M. Grünewald), 1965. (Translation of the French).

——, *Faut-il encore une Liturgie?—Liturgie, Religion et Foi*— (publié sous la direction de) —Coll. Vivante Liturgie 82—Contributions by E. CORNELLIS, A. DOU-TRELOUX, Th. MAERTENS, W. PUTMAN, Paris (Centurion), 1968.

MALINOWSKI, B. *Magic, Science and Religion and Other Essays.* Boston (Beacon Press), 1948 and Glencos, III: The Free Press, 1948 (Also printed in paperback edition by Doubleday Anchor Books, 1954).

MANDERS, H. "Désacralisation de la liturgie" *Paroisse et Liturgie,* Bruges (Abbaye de St. André) (1966), 702-712.

MARTIN, D. *The Religions and the Seculars.* London (Routledge & Kegan Paul), 1969.

MASCALL, E. *The Secularization of Christianity.* New York (Holt, Rinehart & Winston), 1965.

MASURE, E. *Le signe, ou le passage du visible à l'invisible. Psychologie, Histoire, Mystère.* Paris (Bloud & Gay), 1954.

McKENZIE, J.L. "The Word of God in Church and World" XXVII, *North American Liturgical Week,* 72-80.

MEADOWS, P. & MIZMCHI, E.H. *Urbanism, Urbanization and Change. Comparative Perspectives,* Reading Mass. (Addison-Wesley), 1969.

MEERLOO, J.A. *Creativity and Eternization.* Assen, Hetherlands (Van Gorcum), 1967.

MELAND, B.E. *The Secularisation of Modern Cultures.* New York (Oxford University Press), 1963.

METZ, J.B. *Zur Theologie der Welt.* Mainz (M. Grünewald-Verlag), 1968.

——, "Weltverständnis im Glauben—Christliche Orienterung in der Weltlichkeit der Welt heute'' *Geist und Leben* 35, Innsbruck (1962), 165-184.

MODDIE, R. *Brahmanical Culture and Modernity.* Bombay (Asia Publishing House), 1968.

MONEY-KYRLE, E. "The Meaning of Sacrifice" *The International Psycho-Analytic Library*, Nr. 16; London (Hogarth Press), 1930.

MORAN, G. "The Theology of Secularity: What happened to Worship", *Worship in the City of Man*, XXVII—North American Liturgical Week-Houston —Texas, 1966; Washington D.C. (Liturgical Conference) 1966, 80-90.

MOWINCKEL, S. *Religion und Kultus.* Göttingen, 1953 (translation of *Religion oq Kultur*, Oslo, 1950).

MUBENGAYI, P.C. "La choréographie bantoue: Un patrimoine d'équilibre psychologique", *Mitte me*, Roma, Nr. 2 (1962) 13-22.

MUMFORD, L. *The Myth of the Machine—Technics and Human Development*, N. York (Hancourt, G. & Wuld), 1967.

MUNBY, D. *The Idea of a Secular Society.* London (Oxford University Press), 1963.

MURDOCK, R. *Social Structure.* New York (Macmillan) 1949.

NEALE, R.E. *In Praise of Play.* New York (Harper & Row) 1969.

NEUNHEUSER, B. *Opfer Christi und Opfer der Kirche.* Düsseldorf (Patmos-Verlag) 1960.

NEWBIGIN, L. *Honest Religion for Secular Man.* London (SCM) 1966.

NICHOLE, J.H. *History of Christianity 1650-1950: Secularisation of the West.* New York (Ronald Press Co.) 1956.

OHM, Th. *Die Gebetsgelbärden der Völker und das Christwentum.* Leiden (Brill), 1948.

O'HANLON, D. "The Secularity of Christián Worship", *Worship in the City of Man*, XXVII, North American Liturgical Week. Houston—Texas, 1966. Washington (The Liturgical Conference), 16-28.

PANIKKAR, R. "Le Concept d'Ontonomie" *Actes du XIème. Congrès International de Philosophie*, Vol. III, Bruxelles, 1953.

——, "La Misa como 'Consecratio Temporis'. La Tempiternidad" *Proceedings of the Congreso Eucarístico Nacional*, Zaragoza (Spain) 1961.

——, *Kultmysterium in Hinduismus und Christentum—Ein Beitrag zur vergleichenden Religions theologie*, Freiburg-München, (Karl Alber), 1964.

——, "The Internal Dialogue—The insufficiency of the so-called phenomenological 'epoché' in the religious encounter" *Religion and Society* XV, 3. Bangalore, (September 1968, 55-66).

——, "The People of God and the Cities of Man" in *People and Cities*, edited by S. VERNEY, London (Collins) Fontana Books, 1969, 190-219.

——, *L'homme qui devient Dieu. La foi dimension constitutive de l'homme.* Paris, (Aubier), 1969.

PAQUIER, R. *Traité de liturgique. Le fondément et la structure du culte.* Neuchâtel, Paris (Delacuaux & Niestle) 1965.

PARRINDER, G. *Worship in the World's Religions.* London (Faber & Faber) 1961.

PIEPER, J. "Symbol und Attrappe". *Hochland 36*, Münich, 1938/39.

——, "Verteidigung der Musse; über philosophische Bildung und geistige Arbeit-" Münich, *Hochland*, IV (1947). 209-302.

———, *Musse und Kult.* München (Kösel), 1949.

———, *Leisure, the Basis of Culture.* New York (Pantheon) 1952. (Translation)

——⊢—, *Happiness and Contemplation,* New York (Pantheon) 1958.

———, *Zustimmung zur Welt—Eine Theorie des Festes,* Münster (Kösel) 1963.

PINTO DE OLIVEIRA, C.J. "Advent of Secularization and Revision of the Basis of Morals", *IDO-C,* Rome, Nr. 68-10 (Oct. 3, 1968).

POPPER, K. *Open Society and its Enemies.* London (Routledge & Kegan Paul) 1950.

PRO MUNDI VITA *Festschrift zum Eucharistischen Weltkongress 1960,* München (Max Hueber), 1960.

RAHNER, H. "Die Gottesgeburt", *Zeitschrift fur Kath. Theol.,* Wien, 59 (1935), 377.

———, *Griechische Mythen in christlichen Deutung-Gesammelte Aufsätze.* Zürich (Rhein-Verlag), 1945.

———*Mater Ecclesia. Lobpreis der Kirche aus den ersten Jahrtausend christlichen Literatur* (Benziger) Einsielden, Zürich, 1944.

———, *Die spielende Mensch.* Einsiedeln (Johannes Verlag) 1952.

———, *Man at Play* (English translation). New York (Herder & Herder) 1967.

RAHNER, K. "Theologische Reflexionen zur Säkularisierung" *Schriften zur Theologie,* VIII, (1969) 637-666.

———, *Von der Not und dem Segen des Gebetes.* Insbruck (F.Rauch) 3rd. ed. 1949.

RENDTORFF, T. "Säkularisierung als theologisches Problem" *Neue Zeitsch, f. syst. Theol.,* 4 (1962).

———, "Zur Sakularisierungsproblematik", *Inter. Jahrb. Religionssoziologie,* 2 (1966).

RICHARD, R. *Secularization Theology,* New York, London (Herder), 1967.

ROGERS, C.M. "Worship and Contemporary Asian Man" *Religion and Society,* XVI/2 (June 1969) 51-63. (Bangalore).

ROQUEPLO, Ph. *Expérience du monde: experiénce du Dieu? Récherches Théologiques sur la signification divine des activités humaines,* Paris (Cerf) 1968.

RORDORF, W. *Der Sonntag. Geschichte des Ruhe und Gottesdiensttages im ältesten Christentum.* Abhandlunger fur Theologie des A. und NT, Bd. 43. Zürich-Stuttgart (Zwingli Verlag), 1962.

ROSZAK, Th. *The Making of a Counter Culture.* New York, (Doubleday), 1968.

SCHEIDT, J. "Säkularisierung. Odyssee eines Begriffs". *Hochland,* Münich 58/6 (VIII-66) 347-555.

SCHILLEBEECKX, E. *God the Future of Man* (Translation), N.D. SMITH—New York (Sheed and Ward), 1968.

SCHLETTE, H.R. "Secularization: A Theological Appreciation" *IDO-C,* Rome, Nr. 68-12 (March 28/68).

SCHMAUS, M. & FORSTER, K. (Editors) *Der Kult und der heutige Mensch,* München (Hueber), 1961.

SCHMEMANN, A. *Introduction to Liturgical Theology.* London (Faith Press): Portland, Maine (American Orthodox Press), 1966 .

SCHMIDT, W. "Spiele, Feste, Festepiele", *Paideuma,* Frankfurt, IV (1950) 11-22.

SCHURMANN, H. "Neutestamentliche Marginalien zur Frage des 'Entrakralisierung' ". *Der Seelsorg,* Leipzig, 38 (1938), 38-48; 89-104.

SEBOK, T.A. (Editor) "Myth: A Symposium" *Bibliographical and Special Series,* Nr. 5 (American Folklore Society) Bloomington, 1955.

Bibliography

SHINER, L. "The Concept of Secularization in Empirical Research" *Journal for the Scientific Study of Religions*, VI, 2. New Haven, Washington (Fall 1967) 207-220.

SMITH, H. "Secularization and the Sacred: The Contemporary Scene", in *The Religious Situation: 1968* edited by D.R. CUTLER, Boston (Beacon) 1968, 583-600.

SMITH, R.G. *Secular Christianity.* New York (Harper and Row) 1966.

SPANN, R.J. *Christian Faith and Secularism.* New York (Abingdon Press), 1948.

SPLETT, J. *Sakrament des Wirklichkeit. Vorüberlegungen zu einem weltlichen Begriff des Heiligen, Würzburg, 1968.*

TALLEY, Th. "The Sacredness of Contemporary Worship", XXVII, *North America Liturgical Week,* 28-38.

THOMAS, U. *Staatsallmacht und Ersatzreligion.* München, (Schafer) 1961.

TIMIADES, E. "The Renewal of Orthodox Worship", *Studia Liturgica,* Rotterdam, Vol. VI, Nr. 2.

TURNER, V. *The Forest of Symbols.* Ithaca (Cornell University Press) 1967.

———, *The Ritual Process.* Chicago (Aldine Publ. Co.) 1969.

VAGAGGINI, C. *Il senso teologicao della Liturgia—Saggio di liturgia teologica generale*—Roma (Edizione Paoline), 1957.

VANBERGEN, P. "Le culte rendu à Dieu dans une époque sécularisée", *Verbum Caro,* Neuchatel, XXII (1968), Nr. 1968, 48.82.

VATICAN Council II. Decret: 'De Liturgia'.

WARNACH, V. "Kirche und Kosmos. Enkainia", *Gesammelte Arbeiten zum 800 jährigen Weihegedächtnis der Abteikirche Maria Laach*, Maria Laach, 24/VIII/1956.

WASHINGTON, J. *Black Religion.* Boston (Beacon Press) 1966.

WEAKLAND, R.G. "Worship in a Secular World", *IDO-C*, Rome, (Editorial Note) Nr. 68-11; March 17/68.

WECKWERTH, A. "Tisch und Altar. Eine gruendsätzliche Erwägung", *Zeitsch. f. Religions und Geistesgeschichte.* Leiden (Brill), XV, 3 (1963), 209-244.

WEIDKUHN, P. *Agressivität, Ritus, Säkularisierung.* Basel (Pharos) 1965.

WEIL, S. *Pensées sans ordre concernant l'amour de Dieu,* Paris (Gallimard), 1962.

WEINER, M. (Editor) "Modernization: The Dynamics of Growth", *Voice of America Forum Lectures,* 1966.

WENSCHKEWITZ, H. *Die Spiritualisierung der Kultusbegriffe, Tempel, Priester und Opfer im N.T., N.T.,* Leipzig, 1932

WHITE, J.F. *The Worldliness of Worship.* New York (Oxford University Press), 1967.

WHITEHEAD, A.N. *Symbolism.* New York (G.P. Putnam's Sons), 1927.

WILL, R. *Le Culte.* 3 vols. Paris, Strasbourg, 1925-1935.

WILSON, B.R. *Religion in a Secular Society.* London, (Watts & Co. Books), 1966.

WRITING, J.W.M. "The Cross Cultural Method" GARDER LINDZEY, (Ed.) *Handbook of Social Psychology*Vol. I, 523-531, Cambridge (Addison-Wesley), 1954.

YERKES, R.K. *Sacrifice in Greek and Roman Religions and early Judaism.* New York (Scribner's), 1952.

YOUNG, K. *The Drama of the Medieval Church.* Cambridge (Cambridge Univ. Press) 2 vols., 1933.

ZELLER, H. *Und Morgen ist Sonntag.* Münster (Ars Sacra) 1959.